ST CROSS COLLEGE
at Fifty

ST CROSS COLLEGE
at Fifty

Jan-Georg Deutsch
Diarmaid MacCulloch
and Tim Pound

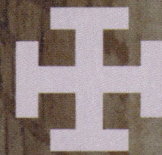

Edited by **Emilie Savage-Smith**
Foreword by **Mark Jones**

First published in 2014 by St Cross College
61, St Giles
Oxford OX1 3LZ
www.stx.ox.ac.uk

Hardback ISBN: 978-0-9930099-0-7
Paperback ISBN: 978-0-9930099-1-4

Designed by Isobel Gillan
Print management by IMAGO
Printed and bound in China

British Library Catalogue in Publishing Data
A CIP record of this publication is available from the British Library.

Cover images: (front) Armillary sphere sundial in west quad of St Giles
site © Dick Makin. (back) The founding fellows © Jeremy Moeran,
Studio Edmark. The Old School House and hut on St Cross Road site
and the garden in west quad of St Giles site © St Cross Archives.

CONTENTS

FOREWORD 7

Mark Jones

THE FOUNDATION YEARS: 1965–1979 12

Tim Pound

GROWING ON A NEW SITE: 1979–1996 64

Diarmaid MacCulloch

A FEELING OF PERMANENCE: 1996–2014 110

Jan-Georg Deutsch

Acknowledgements 146

Sources and Suggested Reading 149

Index of Personal Names 151

Subscribers 156

Photograph Credits 160

FOREWORD

When it was founded in 1965 St Cross was not just a new college but a new kind of college, responding to the emergence of subjects that had not traditionally been taught in Oxford and to the increasing importance for the University of research and in particular of scientific research. And yet its creation, to bring together and provide a proper place within the University for those doing research in and teaching new subjects who had no college fellowship, was also the reassertion of a tradition that values collegiality and participation in University governance.

There was nothing grand about this new institution. Housed in a wooden hut, informal and egalitarian, it did not conform to received ideas of an Oxbridge college. But it achieved the essential: a convivial communal life and enjoyable opportunities for discussing and exchanging ideas across disciplines and cultures.

Bit by bit St Cross also became a significant graduate college. Few in number at first, the College now has over 500 students from every subject and from all over the world. Individually and collectively students and fellows make a notable contribution to Oxford's reputation as a great international research university. And St Cross students have gone on to achieve distinction around the globe, forming an ever stronger network of alumni, united by their affection for the College and their time in Oxford.

What is the role of a graduate college in the twenty-first century? Not to emulate the development of the older colleges which gradually

The entrance to St Cross College, shared with Pusey House, on St Giles Street, 2013.

took over teaching and some aspects of research from the University – the ever more specialised and resource-hungry nature of many disciplines in the twenty-first century thankfully rules that out. Rather to provide a valuable complement and counterpart to the role of University departments by catering to the human and intellectual needs which they cannot meet: the need to feel part of a community, various in interest and outlook, that can eat together and play together. A community that offers places to live and people to meet and which prevents minds from narrowing in the pursuit of knowledge by encouraging discussion and friendship across disciplines.

Moving to Pusey House, building new accommodation and expanding its numbers, has helped St Cross to work better for all its members. But there is no doubt that more is needed. Before too long I hope the college will have significantly more people living on site, with more places to study and meet around its lovely garden.

The garden in the west quad on the St Giles site, 2013.

OVERLEAF: A view of
the Blackwell Quad
looking toward the
chapel of Pusey
House, 2013.

This book is not a history of St Cross, more a reminiscence, after fifty years, of the road travelled so far and a reconnection with all of those, living and dead, who have played a part in making St Cross the place it has been and the place it is today. We owe great thanks to all who have contributed their memories and images, to the triumvirate of authors Jan-Georg Deutsch, Diarmaid MacCulloch and Tim Pound who have made the story of the College and its members come to life, and above all to Emilie Savage-Smith who has been the most wonderfully percipient, patient and persistent editor and who has so brilliantly brought this book into being.

I hope that *St Cross College at Fifty* will give pleasure to all those who have had the privilege of being part of this College over the past half century and that it may provide a point of reference, and in that sense a foundation, for the achievements of our successors.

MARK JONES, Master

THE FOUNDATION YEARS
1965–1979

Tim Pound

During the decades following the end of the First World War, the University of Oxford experienced some of the most radical systemic changes in its long and eventful history. While its collegiate structure would emerge from the war years virtually unchanged, the diverse needs of a modern, post-war economy coupled with the expansion of higher education in general meant that Oxford's exclusive focus on the education of a privileged undergraduate minority could no longer be sustained. As one historian of the University, Jose Harris, has succinctly put it, the University had effectively reached the point where it was obliged to look beyond its traditional role of functioning solely as 'a nursery for citizens and gentlemen.'

This transitional state of affairs came about for several reasons. First, the establishment of four academic halls for women before the turn of the century (Lady Margaret Hall 1878, Somerville 1879, St Hugh's 1886 and St Hilda's 1893) marked the beginning of the end of centuries of masculine domination. These embryonic colleges came into existence through the persistent efforts of a number of enlightened individuals determined to ensure that women should enjoy the same benefits provided by an Oxford education as their male counterparts. As we shall see, their *modus operandi*, resulting in the establishment of a representative body called 'The Association for Promoting the Higher Education of Women', provides a striking parallel to the activities of the non-fellows' movement of the 1960s whose campaign for recognition within the University would later prove to be instrumental in the

A view across the Blackwell Quad from the Four Colleges Archway, St Giles site, 2013.

establishment of new graduate colleges. Although women were initially prevented from participating fully in university life and were not permitted to graduate with an Oxford BA in the pre-war years, the fact that they finally achieved full membership of the University in 1920 effectively set a precedent for further institutional reforms.

Secondly, the increasing importance of science and technology gave rise to a number of questions about the relevance of Oxford's academic curriculum, and in particular, the pre-eminent position enjoyed by *literae humaniores* or classical studies. Aptly credited with being 'the organising principle of pre-war Oxford', *literae humaniores* provided a staggering seventy per cent of all those graduating with a first-class degree during the first four decades of the twentieth century.

Despite the fact that the study of the classics had become virtually synonymous with the concept of an 'Oxford education', even before hostilities in Europe ceased in 1918 the University had already made significant contributions to the war effort through the pioneering work of its scientists. It had also begun to respond to the needs of industry, commerce and the professions by establishing new degree courses in engineering, the sciences (both applied and natural) and clinical medicine. These innovative measures would ultimately pave the way for a fairly dramatic reconfiguration of the balance between the arts and sciences. Perhaps more significantly, they contributed towards the gradual expansion of graduate study and research.

> *Despite the fact that the study of the classics had become virtually synonymous with the concept of an 'Oxford education', even before hostilities in Europe ceased in 1918 the University had already made significant contributions to the war effort through the pioneering work of its scientists.*

Of even greater significance to the growth of science and the expansion of graduate research in general was the introduction of the DPhil degree in 1917. Initially dismissed by some of its opponents as that 'distasteful medium of dry Teutonic pedantry', the DPhil, together with the BLitt introduced at the end of the nineteenth century, provided a much-needed boost to graduate study and research across all subject areas in Oxford in the years leading up to the outbreak of the Second World War.

Last but by no means least, in tandem with the growth of science, the early decades of the twentieth century also witnessed a concomitant expansion in the breadth of arts and social science subjects offered by the University. The introduction of new academic disciplines such as modern and oriental languages, geography, anthropology, economics, psychology and physiology, gave rise to a further expansion in the numbers applying for graduate degrees. For example, during the academic year 1938–39, the number of graduate students in the University stood at 536 – little more than ten per cent of the entire student population – but twenty-five years later (1964) this figure had risen substantially to 2,153 or approximately one quarter of Oxford's entire student population.

The collegiate system at breaking point

Throughout all the changes outlined above, however, the focus of Oxford's academic life remained rooted in its collegiate structure and firmly centred on the education of a privileged undergraduate community. Small wonder, then, as the Franks Report would tellingly reveal, that the majority of Oxford's growing population of graduate students felt decidedly alienated from the communal traditions of the Colleges to which they were attached. The reasons for this were varied. Graduate students tended to be older than their undergraduate contemporaries and were often married, some with young families. Thus, while they had equal access to the facilities enjoyed by their undergraduate contemporaries – such as the use of a College library, involvement in a College's sporting activities and dining in Hall – many felt isolated and marginalised within communities that had evolved historically to cater for the needs of their undergraduate members. This sense of alienation was perhaps most acutely felt by non-Oxford graduates who arrived at the University largely unprepared for the prevailing ethos of collegiate life. By the late 1950s, however, some Colleges had begun to offer their graduate applicants a separate, communal meeting place – the 'Middle Common Room' – Lincoln being the first to do so in 1958. Nonetheless, by the mid-1960s, a mere fifteen per cent of graduate students were housed in College accommodation.

Graduate students, however, were by no means the only members of the University to feel marginalised within Oxford's collegiate environment. A growing number of academic staff not only found themselves denied College fellowships but their subsequent involvement in College life could at best be described as tenuous. Those recruited to teach the emergent disciplines that were attracting Oxford's expanding graduate population tended to be specialists in subject areas that held little intrinsic value for a collegiate system predicated on the teaching of undergraduate students. Moreover, despite the establishment of five new Colleges during the post-war period – two specialised graduate Colleges, Nuffield (1958) and St Antony's (1948); the graduate society Linacre House (1962), and two 'mixed' Colleges accepting both undergraduate and graduate students, St Anne's and St Catherine's – by the early 1960s, out of a total University population of 986 academic and research staff, only 560 held College fellowships. Thus with over forty per cent of its senior membership without any formal affiliation to a College, Oxford had reached a critical point in its history. What was effectively at stake was its very existence as a collegiate university.

The plight of the 'non-dons'

Towards the end of September 1961, a group of non-fellows – or 'non-dons' as they became more popularly known – decided to convene an informal meeting intended to raise the profile of the non-fellowship issue within the University. Among those who attended were a number of non-dons who would become founding fellows of St Cross. According to one account, it was Marshall Macdonald ('Mac') Spencer, Secretary of the then Institute of Education and later a fellow of St Cross, who seized the opportunity afforded by the meeting to speculate somewhat presciently on the chances of 'getting a new graduate college founded in Oxford for the purpose of absorbing non-dons as fellows, and graduates as students for higher degrees.' Also present at this historic gathering was William Edward van Heyningen, a scientist of South African descent and at that time a Senior Research Officer in the School of Pathology. Known to friends and colleagues alike as 'Kits', he would later find himself being appointed the first Master of St Cross College.

What united the non-don faction went beyond a shared sense of professional frustration over their lack of entitlement to the usual privileges associated with College membership, such as the benefit of full dining rights or the added bonus of a College stipend to supplement their University salary. Although the absence of such privileges clearly rankled, their principal grievances arose from their total lack of influence over policy-making within the very University that employed them, and their exclusion from the micro-political world of College affairs, such as the selection of students.

Kits van Heyningen on the plight of the 'non-dons' before 1965, as recorded in his booklet 'The Founding of St Cross College':

Those who are not College Fellows are given little say in University administration or in such vital matters as the admission of students whom they subsequently have to teach. They are hardly ever appointed to University Committees; they have not even been appointed to the Committee on the relationship between the University and Colleges. There is also an anomaly in the distribution of Fellowships among subjects; Fellowships are particularly sparse among subjects which do not have large numbers of honours students. The lack of amenities too is serious. Some of those engaged in teaching are not even provided with any accommodation for the purpose. Many have no common room facilities. This does not only imply that they have nowhere to entertain but, far more important, they lack the means of making contact with their colleagues in other Faculties.

Against the backdrop of a more general enquiry into the relationship between the University and Colleges authorised by the University's governing body (at that time called the Hebdomadal Council) and conducted by a committee chaired by Oxford's then Vice-Chancellor, A.L.P. Norrington, President of Trinity College, the non-dons agreed to hold further meetings during the early part of Michaelmas Term of 1961 to discuss the issue of College affiliation.

As their movement began to gather more support and their membership grew, the non-dons became more formally organised. At a public meeting held on 15 November 1961, a 'Committee of

Non-Fellows' was established. Its executive function was to represent to others the views of the non-fellows' movement as a whole and Kits van Heyningen was invited to serve as its *ex officio* chairman. Richard Freeborn, a University Lecturer in Russian who subsequently left Oxford to take up a professorial chair in London, was elected as secretary. Within a matter of weeks of its formation, this newly-established committee had drafted a memorandum drawing attention to the inequalities experienced by full-time academic staff without College membership, the extent of the disaffection these had caused, and the likely consequences for the University. An amended version was sent to the Vice-Chancellor, Norrington, with a request that its contents be considered by Hebdomadal Council's committee examining the relationship between the University and the Colleges. By this means, the plight of the non-dons reached the highest level of the University's administrative hierarchy, and from this point onwards, it seemed, their grievances could no longer be ignored by the University authorities.

The University's response, however, was decidedly slow in coming and when Norrington finally wrote to van Heyningen some months later in March, 1962, his reply must have come as a disappointment. In essence he declared he had 'nothing to report' on the issue of integrating academic staff without fellowships into the College system, but conceded that this had resulted not from 'any lack of goodwill' but from an 'inability to find an agreed basis of action.'

Undeterred, the Committee of Non-Fellows then wrote to the University Registrar, Sir Folliott Sandford, a supporter of the non-dons' cause, urging him to press for some form of representation on the Norrington Committee. On this occasion, however, the University's response, conveyed in a personal letter from Norrington himself, was far more encouraging. Exceeding most, if not all, of Kits van Heyningen's expectations, the text of the letter concluded with the following proposal: 'the best way to get rapid and effective results would be to set up a special sub-committee consisting of three of their own members and two members of your group, to assemble the facts and report, as soon as possible, to the main Committee.'

Having been invited to serve on this sub-committee, Kits van Heyningen promptly resigned his chairmanship of the Committee of Non-Fellows, in order, as he put it, 'to distance myself from the non-dons for the time being.' His role as chairman was then filled by Tom Tinsley, a microbiologist, who would later become a fellow of St Cross.

Although the bureaucratic wheels of the University turned slowly, as far as the association of non-fellows was concerned, they were finally moving in the right direction. In fact, the newly-appointed sub-committee, chaired by Robin Harrison – soon to be elected Warden of Merton College – made remarkable progress. Between its formation in May and the publication of its findings in November of 1962, Harrison's Committee met on fifteen separate occasions, and once its report had been submitted, copies were circulated across the University and responses to its recommendations collated and then forwarded to the Norrington Committee.

The sub-committee reported to the Hebdomadal Council:

Our proposals, very briefly, are that all members of the graduate staff of the University ought to have some form of affiliation with some form of graduate society, that this cannot be fully achieved without the creation of new societies (and the expansion of certain existing ones), but that homes could and should be found for many within the existing colleges. We make these proposals in the firm conviction that the members of the academic staff of a collegiate university (the merits of which we have not thought necessary to argue) should have the opportunity of participating in something more than a '9 to 5 job' in the university department in which they are primarily employed. As things are, however, a large number of the academic staff of this university are not given any such opportunity, and, if the University expands much farther without anything being done, they will form the majority. If they do, then Oxford will cease to be a collegiate university and will become instead a university to which some colleges are affiliated; our proposals are designed to prevent this from ever happening.

Once it became clear that the issue of College affiliation would never be resolved through what amounted to a form of centralised coercion, the non-fellows' movement began to concentrate its energies on the principal recommendation of Harrison's Committee: the establishment of new graduate societies. In April 1963, the views of more than two hundred non-fellows were canvassed, and it soon became evident that a considerable majority endorsed the foundation of a new graduate College. As one of its members, Richard Freeborn, observed at the time: 'there is a genuine feeling among both non-fellows and graduate students that, because they are officially outside the College system, they can only enjoy a "second-best" Oxford. A new graduate College would meet the need for fellowship, both academically and socially, which the present undergraduate Colleges cannot provide.'

By now well-versed in the tactical business of establishing new committees to expedite a cause, in June 1963 the non-fellows elected a further sub-group called the 'Promotion Committee' to spearhead its campaign for the foundation of a new graduate College. Members of this committee, including Kits van Heyningen, then met to argue their case with the newly appointed Vice-Chancellor, Walter Oakeshott, Rector of Lincoln College. While it soon became clear that no University funds were available to endow the building of new graduate societies on the scale of St Antony's or Nuffield, Oakeshott was broadly sympathetic to the suggestion that the Promotion Committee ought to approach potential benefactors outside the University. He also warmed to the idea of the Promotion Committee making a direct appeal to some of the richer Oxford Colleges for financial support, a strategy which would eventually have a considerable bearing on the founding of St Cross some two years later.

In January of 1964 the Norrington Committee finally submitted its own findings. Its report proved to be a most influential document, not least because it acknowledged the fact that Oxford had reached a critical point in its evolution and formally conceded that 'the main business of the University' was no longer 'the teaching of undergraduates.' What was of paramount importance, it argued, was a resolution of the non-fellowship issue, since the tenure of a fellowship conferred upon its holder a certain status for which 'any substitute would be an inferior imitation.' As for those involved in graduate teaching, however, the report was adamant that their 'absorption into the existing colleges … is neither feasible or desirable', and it concluded: 'We are in no doubt that the right solution to the problem of the integration of this class into the college system is the foundation of new collegiate societies.'

By February of that year Congregation had approved, virtually without exception, the policies embodied in the Norrington Report, and as a result, Hebdomadal Council appointed a further committee, once again with Norrington in the chair, to make detailed recommendations for their implementation. The committee was supplemented by the Principal of Linacre House and two prominent members of the non-fellows' movement: Kits van Heyningen, who now enjoyed the distinction of being the first non-fellow to be elected as a member of Hebdomadal Council; and Alan Jones, a Lecturer in Oriental Studies, who would later serve as the first Vice-Master of St Cross.

The following month, the Committee of Non-Fellows, under the guidance of Tom Tinsley, voted in favour of transforming itself into 'The Oxford Collegiate Society.' Having completed this strategic realignment, the new Society then set about the task of petitioning Hebdomadal Council for University recognition, and perhaps more significantly, a permanent base in which to meet and conduct its affairs.

Meanwhile, in a related development, the Registrar, Sir Folliott Sandford, had asked Jack Lankester, then University Surveyor, to assess the suitability of two potential locations for the establishment of new graduate societies. The first was 10 St Cross Road, a comparatively small site of around three-quarters of an acre comprising a Victorian vicarage, a schoolhouse and caretaker's lodge. Having recently housed the Institute of Economics and Statistics, this was regarded as a good location and conveniently situated for the University's libraries and science departments. The second was Court Place, Iffley, a well-preserved eighteenth-century house set in more than eight acres of grounds, but located over two miles from the centre of the city.

Financial estimates covering capital expenditure for furnishings, alterations and repairs together with running costs were also set out. There was one additional, yet crucial, development: four of the wealthiest Colleges agreed to provide a capital sum of £29,000 and an annual grant of £18,000 over a period of ten years to help fund the costs associated with the establishing and initial running of the two graduate Colleges.

> *Four of the wealthiest colleges had agreed to provide a capital sum of £29,000 and an annual grant of £18,000 over a period of ten years to help fund the costs associated with establishing and initial running of the two postgraduate colleges.*

By February 1965, the foundation of the two Colleges moved a stage closer when the Norrington Committee submitted draft statutes for each of the new graduate communities. In a separate proposal, it was also suggested that each College should initially assume the name of its location, in other words that of 'St Cross' and 'Iffley', but that these should be considered as provisional only. By the following month, a letter had been dispatched to all non-dons considered eligible for membership in the proposed Colleges, asking recipients to confirm which of the two graduate societies they preferred to join. Provisional lists were then drawn up and some adjustments made to ensure that numbers were balanced and that the fellowship of each College represented a similar range of subject disciplines.

All that remained was the appointment of the two Principals. To oversee this process, Hebdomadal Council commissioned a further committee including Norrington and Harrison, which met during Trinity Term of 1965 to consider suitable candidates. After several weeks of deliberation and consultation, the committee eventually offered the post of Principal of St Cross College to Kits van Heyningen, which he accepted. Some months later, Hebdomadal Council confirmed the appointment of Isaiah Berlin as Principal-designate of Iffley.

Having been an active participant in the non-fellows' association from the outset and, as we have seen, chair of several key committees that proved instrumental in advancing its cause, Kits van Heyningen's appointment ensured that during its early, foundation years the College would develop under the guidance of someone who not only understood the needs and aspirations of its senior membership, but also its role in establishing a supportive and stimulating intellectual environment in which its graduate students could flourish.

Much had thus been achieved in the relatively brief period of time that had elapsed since the non-fellows gathered for their very first meeting in September, 1961. Expectations were understandably high, but before St Cross College could commence its operations as a fully-functioning graduate College of the University – though technically with the status of a University Department until an endowment could be obtained allowing full independence – some essential formalities had to be completed before its inauguration, not least an official confirmation of its fellowship. Before the start of Michaelmas Term, 1965, legislation establishing the foundation of both St Cross College and Iffley College had already been put before Congregation by Oakeshott's successor as Vice-Chancellor, Kenneth Wheare, where it passed without opposition. Then on 20 September the *Oxford University Gazette* published an announcement from Hebdomadal Council stating it had 'designated the following persons as Official Fellows of St Cross College and Iffley College respectively, with effect from 1 October 1965', followed by a list of the founding fellows of each of the two Colleges. Thus it was that 1 October would mark the official foundation of the College.

What's in a name?

In his autobiography published in 1987, Kits van Heyningen revealed how the name 'St Cross' – one that has undeniably endeared itself to all those who have been associated with the College during the last fifty years – could so easily have become elided from its history at the very moment of its foundation. The reasons for this lay in the fact that as the Head of House of a new Oxford College, van Heyningen was acutely aware he would need to attract a substantial endowment to secure its future. In this context, the idea of re-naming the College after one of the many distinguished Oxford alumni seemed a shrewd strategic move. Given his scientific background, his first thoughts quite naturally turned to such eminent figures as Robert Boyle, Robert Hooke, or even Christopher Wren, the astronomer and mathematician more generally revered for his architectural legacy. That his ruminations also took a decidedly idiosyncratic turn is evinced by his decision to make a personal appeal for funding to none other than the Queen of the Netherlands. Irrespective of whether or not his Dutch ancestry had some bearing on this rather ambitious petition, had it proved successful the University could well have admitted 'Queen Juliana College' into its ranks rather than St Cross.

As we shall see, St Cross would once again risk the loss of its name at a further stage in its history during negotiations over its relocation to its current home in St Giles. Nonetheless, the College's identity has remained resolutely linked to the name of the site on which it originated. Its location on what is now St Cross Road originally lay outside the city walls and close to a 'holy well' in a sparsely populated area that was known as Holywell Greene or Common. The adjacent church dates from the eleventh century. Originally built as a chapel and dedicated to the holy cross, it took the name 'Holywell' from its location, though later the name of the church was changed to Holy Cross before becoming more popularly (but unofficially) known as St Cross Church during the nineteenth century. The nearby

Detail of the Holywell area from the map published in 1675 by David Loggan, titled *Nova & Accuratissima Celeberrimae Universitatis Civitatisque Oxoniensis Scenographia*. The future location of the 'hut' of St Cross College is indicated in red.

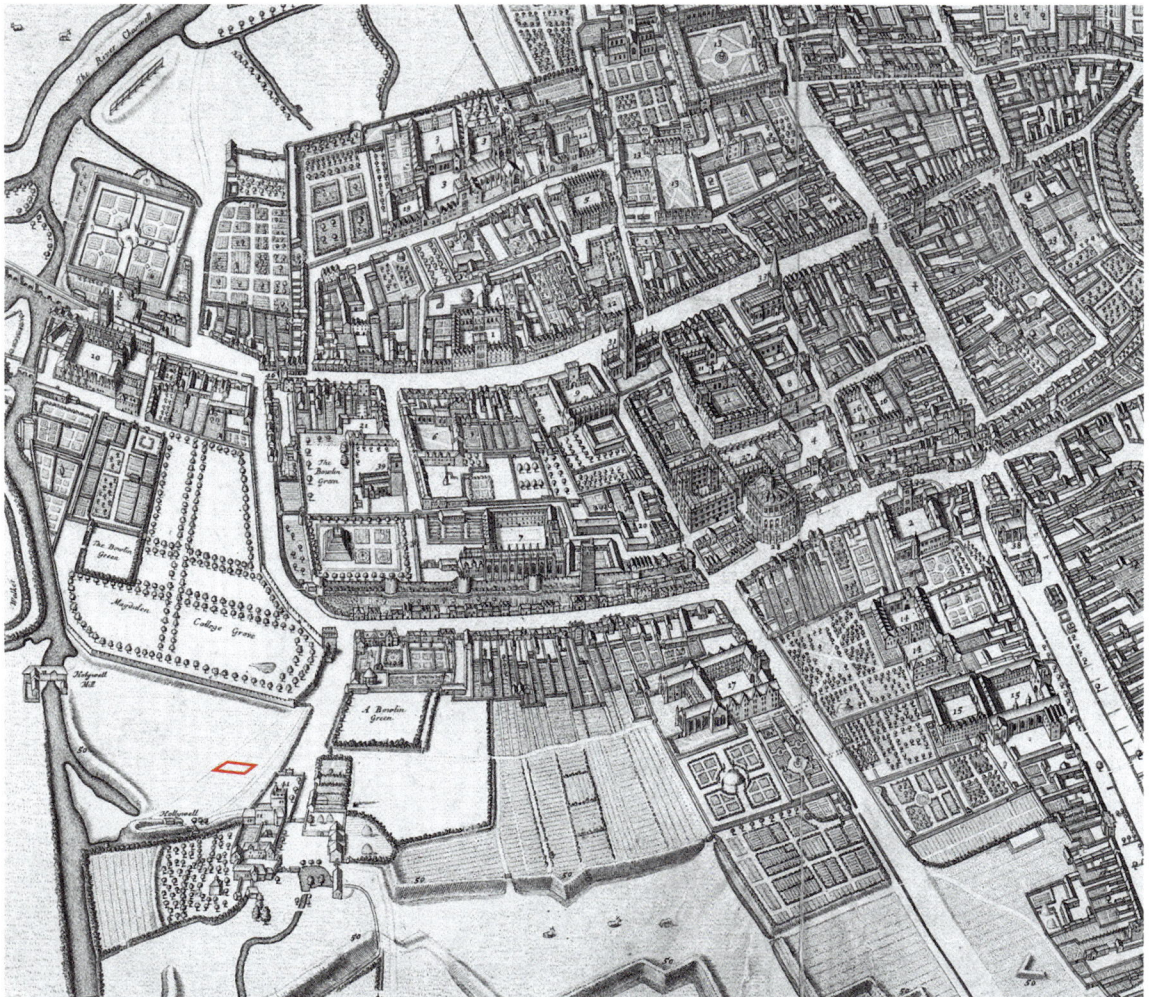

W

N

Holywell Church in an engraving by J. Le Keux after a lithograph by F. Mackenzie, printed in 1835.

Manor House, together with a mill straddling a tributary stream from the River Cherwell, dates from roughly the same period as the church. These buildings were the most prominent features of what remained an essentially rural area throughout the middle ages until the present Manor House was rebuilt at the beginning of the sixteenth century. By this time Holywell Greene included a cockpit and a gallows, together with a pillory and stocks, the latter probably located at the junction of what is now Longwall Street and St Cross Road.

One of the earliest maps of the area, published by Ralph Agas in 1577, shows Holywell Lane (not Street) and The Long Walk (the precursor of Long Wall Street) but there is no indication of what would become St Cross Road. David Loggan's map, which first appeared towards the end of the seventeenth century, reveals that further changes had taken place including the construction of a number of houses on the north side of Holywell Lane opposite Magdalen College Grove together with several other dwellings to the west of Holywell Church. By the middle of the eighteenth century, according to a street plan of the city published in *The New Oxford Guide* in 1759, Holywell Lane had become Holywell Street, and what is now a clearly delineated road running north from the junction of Holywell Street and Long Walk towards the church had been given the name Holywell Lane.

By the early nineteenth century more distinctive transformations had taken place. As the charming engraving of Holywell Church by J. Le Keux, printed in 1835, suggests, the parish of Holywell had by this time become considerably more urbanised and Holywell Lane (the forerunner of St Cross Road) now appears to have a cobbled surface.

Detail from the Ordnance Survey map of 1876 (scale 1:2,500), with the future location of the 'hut' indicated in red.

During the course of the century, as shown in the first Ordnance Survey map of the area published in 1876, the parish of Holywell would be subjected to further changes. Firstly, on the site that would eventually be occupied by St Cross College, a vicarage had been erected to the south of the church. Nearby stood two school buildings, one of which was attached to a small lodge built to accommodate the caretaker of an adjoining cemetery that opened in the 1840s to ease pressure on the availability of burial plots in the city. What became the north porch of the new lodge originally served as separate lych-gate to the cemetery before it was attached to the external wall of the lodge in 1848. Additionally, a more subtle transformation appears to have taken place – Holywell Church has now become designated as Holy Cross Church, although Holywell Lane remains unchanged, and the adjacent Manor House, which had earlier served as a workhouse, has become a female penitentiary. The name Holy Cross continued in use alongside the older Holywell for both the church itself and the adjacent cemetery until the church was closed in 2008 and converted into the Balliol Historic Collections Centre. By the end of the nineteenth century, however, the popular common name for the church became St Cross Church,

LEFT: The north porch of the new lodge originally served as a separate lych-gate to the cemetery before it was attached to the external wall of the lodge in 1848.

RIGHT: The Victorian vicarage, ca 1964, shortly before its demolition.

rather than Holy Cross or Holywell, and the lane alongside became St Cross Road. Apart from the closure of the two schools due to dwindling numbers just before the start of the Second World War, coupled with the fact that the vicarage had gradually fallen into a state of disrepair since it had been unoccupied for some years, the three-quarters-of-an-acre site adjacent to St Cross Church would remain substantially untouched until the University purchased it from its owners, Merton College, on behalf of St Cross College in 1965.

Preparing the site

In February of 1965, the Norrington Committee invited Kits van Heyningen to join a sub-committee tasked with preparing an architect's brief for adapting the existing buildings on the St Cross site to house the new College. Following the advice of the University Surveyor, Jack Lankester, a decision was taken to demolish the Victorian vicarage since it was ravaged by death-watch beetle and dry-rot and the cost of its restoration was deemed to be financially prohibitive. It was also decided

The Common Room in the hut on St Cross Road, *ca* 1970.

BELOW: The interior of the Old School House refurbished to serve as the library and meeting room for the Governing Body, *ca* 1970.

that the smaller of the two school rooms on the north-east corner of the site should be razed and replaced by a temporary wooden building or 'hut', as it became affectionately known. Kits' personal brief for the new building was fairly modest. It should be large enough to accommodate a sizeable Common Room in addition to a general office, a separate room for the Principal, a small kitchen and cloakrooms.

Kits van Heyningen on the essentials for a new College:

I had only one difference with Jack Lankester [the University Surveyor]. Space being short, he wanted to put one cubicle each in the men's and women's lavatories. I said to him 'Dammit Jack, I can't tell my friends in the Reform Club I'm Principal of a two-bog college in Oxford.' So we had five, three in the women's and two and a thingummy in the men's.

The Old School House, later called the Kirby Old School, in a pencil drawing by F. R. Wigston, 1982.

Given the restricted size of the proposed structure – the hut itself would measure approximately eighty feet by thirty – the creation of a separate hall was out of the question, and it was agreed that only a simple lunch would be provided throughout the week in the Common Room, thus preserving, as van Heyningen put it, 'the custom of lunching together that had been established by the Oxford Collegiate Society.' Further alterations were subsequently approved including the refurbishment of the schoolhouse to serve as a College library and meeting room, and the renovation of the lodge to provide accommodation for a cook/housekeeper or College porter. The schoolhouse, a handsome stone building built in the Victorian Gothic style, had been designed by the well-known Oxford architect Charles Buckeridge. It was completed in 1858 and replaced a smaller and slightly earlier schoolroom designed by Thomas Grimsley in 1850. Grimsley's original lodge, however, was preserved, not least because the building made use of an innovative technique in which terracotta tiles, rather than timber, were used in the gable ends to support the roof.

The wooden hut and Old School House with newly created parking lot. July 1966.

Although both the schoolroom and the attached lodge were fairly modest stone buildings by Oxford standards, their presence on the original site, together with their close proximity to the church, enabled the new College to acquire from the outset a veneer of historical respectability. In fact, considerable care was devoted to the restoration of both buildings. For example, when a number of terracotta tiles on the lodge were discovered to be either broken or missing, the artist John Piper, later elected an Honorary Fellow of St Cross, was commissioned to produce exact copies, while his life-long friend, the poet John Betjeman, a passionate devotee of all things Victorian, helped to raise the funds to enable the work to be completed.

Once the remains of the vicarage had been completely cleared and the ground levelled and seeded, paving slabs were laid to create a terrace and a car park constructed on the western side of the site bordering St Cross Road. The centrepiece of the newly-seeded lawn was a well-established mulberry tree, appropriately enough an ancient symbol of wisdom, which had been carefully preserved. So too was a more potently

Four fellows in a smoke-filled Common Room following lunch in the hut, *ca* 1970. Kits van Heyningen is at the far right.

emblematic memento from the vicarage itself – a metal cross which had originally surmounted the portico of the building, and which is still reverently displayed in the St Cross Room on our St Giles site. As far as the wooden hut was concerned, it soon became obvious that any attempt to disguise its outline or soften its external appearance would have been pointless. In order to compensate for the drab functionality of its exterior, Kits van Heyningen was determined to make the inside of the building as comfortable as possible. As he would later put it, he wanted to ensure that 'once you were inside the college, you would not know you were in a wooden hut, and it worked.'

Given the absence of a Governing Body at this embryonic stage in the College's history, Kits took personal charge of the hut's transformation during the months leading up to its official opening, choosing furniture and fittings while insisting throughout that there should be no financial compromise over issues of quality and style. For example, orders for furniture were placed with Heal's in London and Gordon Russell in Broadway, wallpaper and curtains were purchased from Sanderson's, while oriental rugs for the polished hardwood floors were bought at auction from Sotheby's. The enduring affection felt by so

The first Master, Kits van Heyningen, in his office in the wooden hut, *ca* 1970.

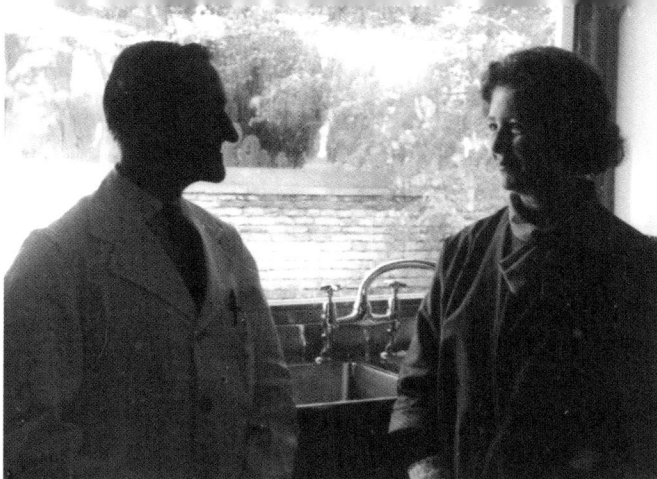

Michael Collins, the College's first porter, with Mrs Collins in the kitchen at the wooden hut.

many senior and junior members of the College towards the wooden hut can, in no small measure, be attributed to the well-appointed and welcoming appearance of its Common Room for which Kits van Heyningen could justifiably claim sole responsibility.

In addition to the task of furnishing both the new and the restored buildings, the recruitment of staff had to be undertaken before the start of the new academic year in October 1965. One such appointment was that of the College's first porter, Mr Michael Collins. Described by Kits van Heyningen as a 'cheeky little man with a cockney accent', at the time of his recruitment he was employed as verger of St Cross Church and lived with his wife in the lodge adjoining the schoolhouse. She too would make an important contribution to the communal life of the College, eventually assuming responsibility for the preparation and serving of lunch in the Common Room.

Kits van Heyningen on our first porter's love of ceremony:

Having adopted St Cross Church as our College Chapel, we decided to have an annual service of thanksgiving in it, and I chose St Crispin's Day for it. I waited in my room while the Fellows and their spouses gathered in the church. When everything was ready, Mr Collins, garbed in his verger's cassock, came to lead me into the church. This necessitated emerging onto the street for a few yards, where some people had gathered to look on. Mr Collins took it upon himself to chant, 'Make way for the Master! Make way for the Master!' all the way from my room to the church, and there was nothing I could do about it.

Getting down to business

Despite the considerable efforts of those involved, however, work on the College site had still to be completed by the start of Michaelmas Term. Thus it was that the founding fellows of St Cross College gathered in Merton College for the first meeting of Governing Body on 5 October 1965, since the buildings on St Cross Road were not yet ready for occupancy. They were forty-four in number, in addition to the Master, and included three women – a most unusual occurrence for the foundation of an Oxford College that was not in origin a women's College. The meeting itself, 'highly charged with triumph and expectancy', was the first of six held that term instead of the usual two – an indication of the sheer range of administrative and policy-making decisions involved in the establishment of a new College. At this inaugural meeting, the first official business was the election of two prominent members of the non-dons' association, Tom Tinsley and 'Mac' Spencer, to Fellowships by Special Election since they had not been in post long enough to be eligible for Official College Fellowships at the time of the foundation of the College. There followed a formal vote of thanks to all those who had contributed, both directly and indirectly, to the founding of the College: the Governing Body of Merton College, both for their general support and for agreeing to make the St Cross Road site available to the University; the Committee of Non-Fellows and the Oxford Collegiate Society; members of the Harrison and the Norrington Committees; and finally, all those Colleges that had provided sufficient capital and endowments to fund the College's foundation, together with Council and Congregation, the University Registrar and University Surveyor, who had lent their support to the project from the outset.

At the second Governing Body meeting held the following week, once again in Merton College, the first Honorary Fellowships of the College were awarded to Robin Harrison, Warden of Merton, and A. L. P. Norrington, President of Trinity College, whose combined pragmatic skills and strategic vision in University affairs had eventually proved instrumental in the founding of St Cross.

Two further issues that would have considerable bearing on the institutional identity of the College were also discussed. The first was the name 'St Cross', which the University had proposed merely as an interim measure. Having considered a number of alternatives, however, Governing Body decided to postpone indefinitely a decision on this issue. The second was the title of 'Principal' for the Head of House. Although there was some support for changing this to 'President', agreement was eventually reached to adopt the title 'Master.'

The first Governing Body meeting, held at Merton College on 5 October 1965. In addition to the thirty-eight people pictured here, seven are absent from the photograph. *Left to Right:* TOP ROW: J.J. MacGregor, H. M. Southern, J.E. Bialokoz, P.H. Nye, D.A.T. Dick, B.A. Coles, J.S. Rollett, S. S. Wilson. SECOND ROW: G.M. Brown, I.G. Philip, D.M. Sutherland, J. Zussman, A.C.R. Dean, K.G.J.C. Knowles, J.E. French, N. Zernov, K.O.L. Burridge. THIRD ROW: A. Ward, H.K. Pusey, G. H. Thompson, R.G. Tucker, F.C. Osmaston, G.P. Gladstone, A.E. Needham, A.G. Antill, W.R.C. Handley, J.A. Spiers. FOURTH/FRONT ROW: J.M. Edmonds, A. Jones, W.H. Beckett, W.T. Davies, M. Marshall, R.E. van Heyningen, The Master (W.E. van Heyningen), R. Barbour, D. Patterson, F.W. Hodcroft, W.A. Gordon. ABSENTEES: D. Britton, T.G. Griffith, C.J.W. Pitt, A.R. Robbins, A.H.T. Robb-Smith, J.M. Todd, A.W. Williams.

At subsequent meetings during that Michaelmas Term, Alan Jones was appointed Vice-Master, with a specific remit to develop the College's links with the University and with other Colleges. Within a year of his appointment, he was invited to join a number of intercollegiate committees and was later elected to the post of University Assessor.

The first Founders' Feast

While the Old School House was able to be used for a Governing Body meeting at the end of November, the 'hut' was not yet fully functional by December of 1965. As a result, the first Founders' Feast of the College had to be held at Trinity College. Pictured here is the menu from this first of many feasts honouring the founders of the College.

The menu of the first Founders' Feast, held 9 December 1965 at Trinity College.

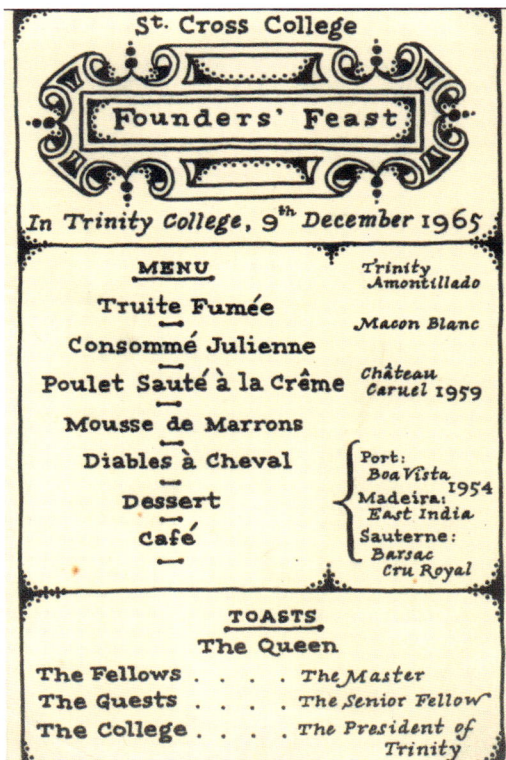

St. Cross College
Founders' Feast
In Trinity College, 9th December 1965

MENU

Truite Fumée — Trinity Amontillado
Consommé Julienne — Macon Blanc
Poulet Sauté à la Crème — Château Caruel 1959
Mousse de Marrons
Diables à Cheval — Port: Boa Vista 1954 / Madeira: East India / Sauterne: Barsac Cru Royal
Dessert
Café

TOASTS

The Queen

The Fellows . . . . . The Master
The Guests . . . . . The Senior Fellow
The College . . . . . The President of Trinity

At the final meeting of what had clearly been a hectic term, Kits van Heyningen informed Governing Body of a number of benefactions to mark the founding of the College. All were gifts of silverware and would effectively form the original core of the College's art collection. These included a salt, pepper and mustard set from Kits van Heyningen's former Cambridge college, Emmanuel, and a silver-gilt cup from Exeter College, where Kits enjoyed Common Room rights following his move from Cambridge in the late 1940s. It was also announced that the Oxford Collegiate Society had donated a fine pair of candlesticks and that Kenelm Burridge, one of the founding fellows of St Cross, had given an épergne. Finally, the College recorded its gratitude to the fellows of Balliol for their donation of an exquisite early nineteenth-century épergne, arguably the most notable gift of all those given to commemorate our foundation.

A pair of silver candlesticks engraved *Presented to the Master and Fellows of St Cross College by the Oxford Collegiate Society, 1965* and presented to the College on 5 November 1965. A second pair was presented at the same time to Iffley College (later to become Wolfson College). These gifts from the College's Founders (that is, the Committee of Non-Fellows which became The Oxford Collegiate Society) were the first items presented to the College on its foundation.

Presented to the Master and Fellows of St Cross College by the members of the Oxford Collegiate Society

Seen in retrospect, these bequests paved the way for what Kits van Heyningen would later refer to as part of the process of creating a 'civilised environment.' In a more general sense, of course, the accumulation of works of art such as these early gifts of silverware also functioned as a visual and material confirmation of the College's newly-emergent status as a *bona-fide* member of an older, and considerably more privileged, academic community. They also proved to be the first of many to enrich the collegiate life of the University's most recent constituent member.

Fundraising and development

As life at College settled into a more recognisable pattern once the frenetic business of the first term had been concluded, Kits van Heyningen's attention inevitably turned to the issue of fundraising to ensure the College's long-term development. In this respect, Iffley College had been more fortunate. Its Principal-designate, the philosopher and political theorist, Isaiah Berlin, had approached both the Ford and Wolfson Foundations for endowments to establish his future College on a secure financial footing. His success in raising a considerable sum from each, however, in effect ensured that the site at Iffley would soon be abandoned in favour of a more centralised location. Thus it was that on the banks of the River Cherwell close to the Banbury Road in North Oxford, the re-named Wolfson College would soon take shape. (Readers will no doubt be intrigued to learn that Wolfson remains in very good hands given the fact that its President since 2008, Professor Dame Hermione Lee, is a St Cross graduate.)

Acutely aware of the need to attract a sizeable benefaction, Kits van Heyningen lost no time during the first few years of the College's existence in scheduling a series of visits targeting potential donors both at home and abroad. Initial redevelopment plans for the site, based upon a conventional quadrangular layout, had in fact already been drawn up by a London-based firm of architects, Stout and Litchfield, as early as August, 1966. While these undeniably succeeded in exploiting to the full the limited scope of the St Cross Road site, their bold and imaginative exterior would provoke mixed reactions. To accompany the architects' plans and sketches of the proposed development, Kits had also compiled a short promotional pamphlet. Appropriately entitled *The Origins and Aims of St Cross College, Oxford*, this document outlined the College's plans for the future, emphasising an initial objective of achieving an Anglo-American bias in its recruitment of graduate students.

Armed with such documentation, van Heyningen embarked on a series of fundraising trips to the USA during the late 1960s. Although he elicited a number of sympathetic responses to the notion of funding a fledgling Oxford College, the large benefaction he had hoped for would remain elusive. There were, however, some incidental consolations, including the bestowal on Kits by the Governor of Dallas of an 'honorary citizenship' of the State of Texas at the instigation, it seems, of his host Frederick Lange. (This distinction was accompanied by the nominal right to the possession of all of one square inch of Texan land.) Of more tangible benefit, however, was a fairly substantial donation from Lewis Kirby, a wealthy businessman from New Jersey. It was Kirby who provided sufficient funds for the restoration and refurbishment of the old Victorian schoolhouse and whose generosity was celebrated by the commissioning of a carved, stone escutcheon displaying his (perhaps fairly notional) coat of arms. Once the restoration work had been

A model of the proposed design for the new College buildings to be built on St Cross Road, produced by the London-based firm Stout & Litchfield, 1966.

The Kirby coat of arms, commemorating the benefactor, Lewis Kirby, who underwrote the restoration of the Old School House on the St Cross Road site. On the right-hand side is the Kirby coat of arms, while that on the left corresponds to no known heraldic design and may have been devised informally to represent the College, with its 'watery' reference to Oxford rivers.

completed, this was placed by the main entrance to the building, which has since retained the name 'Kirby Old School' as a mark of the College's gratitude.

While in the States, Kits van Heyningen had also been introduced to the actor Douglas Fairbanks, Jr. Awarded a knighthood in 1949 for his contribution to the promotion of Anglo-American relations, Fairbanks undoubtedly exuded a blend of glamour and sophistication that one might have expected from a member of Hollywood's elite. In his autobiography, however, Kits concedes that his initial motive in striking up a friendship with the actor had a more pragmatic foundation: that of exploiting Fairbanks' connections with the rich and the powerful in post-war American society, and in particular, Paul Getty. Although Fairbanks would later write to Getty setting out the case for a substantial benefaction by arguing that it would at once enhance the latter's philanthropic reputation whilst enabling the College to secure its future, his appeal for funding was emphatically rebuffed. In fact, Kits' recollection of the gist of Getty's reply to Fairbanks – 'I despise Liberal Arts Colleges … I despise Liberal Arts Students … and I despise Liberal Arts Professors, but out of respect for you I have asked the American Trust Fund to forward $100 to St Cross College' – while exaggerating the tone of Getty's original text, clearly suggests that Getty had little, if any, understanding, let alone appreciation, of Oxford's collegiate history.

As his correspondence with Kits van Heyningen reveals, Fairbanks, on the other hand, would not only prove to be a more generous patron of the College than Getty, but an active supporter of its campaign to attract a substantial benefaction. In July 1968 he was elected to a

Visiting Fellowship at the College. Throughout the period of his College affiliation (1969–1976), Fairbanks visited Oxford and St Cross on a number of occasions, attended Encaenia, and dined both in College and at the home of Kits van Heyningen and his wife Ruth, also a founding fellow of St Cross. Given his international profile and the social and professional whirligig that pervaded his life as a Hollywood celebrity, it is all the more remarkable that Douglas Fairbanks, Jr retained a deep affection for the College that remained undiminished throughout his life. How poignant, therefore, and yet entirely fitting, that in the formal photograph later used in his obituary, he can be seen wearing the earliest version of the College tie.

Although Kits van Heyningen would never manage to secure the sizeable benefaction he had originally hoped for following his visits to the USA, his efforts were not entirely unrewarded. Other donations followed, including a further sum from Kirby himself and an extremely generous amount from John Enders, a Nobel Prize winner and Professor of Bacteriology and Immunology at Harvard Medical School. Yet by far the most enduring legacy of Kits van Heyningen's fundraising activities would, paradoxically, emanate from Oxford itself – from, as Kits put it himself, 'that other great Oxford institution, Blackwell's, the booksellers.'

Kits had first been introduced in the 1950s to the future head of Blackwell Scientific Publications, Per Saugman, who would later play a pivotal role in the College's acquisition of the St Giles site. Saugman was born in Denmark but later moved to the UK where he would spend more than fifty years

The actor Douglas Fairbanks, Jr wearing the earliest version of the St Cross College tie. The photograph appeared in his obituary in *The Daily Telegraph* on 8 May 2000.

of his life. He joined Blackwell Scientific Publications in 1951, rising through the ranks to Managing Director by the time of his retirement in 1987, and in 1989 was awarded an honorary OBE in recognition of his services to publishing. During the early 1960s, as a resident of Harcourt Hill on the western fringes of the city, Per Saugman also became a friend and neighbour of Richard Freeborn, and was thus fully aware of the origins of the non-fellows' movement and no doubt informed of its progress.

Kits also knew the chairman of the parent company, Sir Basil Blackwell, and his son Richard. In fact, shortly after the College had been officially opened, he invited both to lunch in the wooden hut. In his autobiography, van Heyningen recalls how he and his two guests had enjoyed a frank discussion about the College's ambitions to redevelop the St Cross Road site and, in particular, its need to attract a substantial endowment. Shortly after this meeting had taken place, he received a letter from Richard Blackwell at once thanking him for the College's hospitality while nonetheless making it abundantly clear that the company was currently in no position to assist financially. However, somewhat more propitiously, Richard Blackwell had enclosed a cheque for £100, a gesture that van Heyningen interpreted as a potential token of further, and more considerable, financial support.

In this instance Kit's instincts proved right, and before his term as Master of St Cross came to an end, both his percipience and his patience would be amply rewarded by one of the most generous benefactions in the College's history.

Of Richard Blackwell's initial contribution of £100, Kits van Heyningen recalled in his memoirs:

I took that small token very seriously. It was surely not a token of esteem, so I read it as a signal that I should be patient. Over the years I would call on Richard in his office over the shop about once a Term, and sometimes we would touch lightly on the subject of money, and sometimes we would not; but I would always come away with the feeling, almost the knowledge, that I must wait, and one day the money would come.

Life at the St Cross Road site

As soon as the buildings on St Cross Road were available for use in Michaelmas Term of 1965, the communal life of the College began to assume its own distinctive corporate identity. Housed in a comfortably-equipped Common Room strikingly at odds with the rather drab, prefabricated functionality of its exterior, founding fellows and visitors alike could easily convince themselves that they were in more established surroundings.

Described by an early fellow of the College, Eric Whittaker, as having a 'gracious and gentlemanly' interior, the wooden hut was deceptively spacious, for in addition to the Common Room, it incorporated separate office space together with a number of individual pigeon-holes, cloakrooms and a small kitchen in which lunch was prepared throughout the week.

A lunchtime conversation in the hut, ca 1970.

Eric Whittaker in his 'Recollections of a Hut Dweller' recalls those early days:

Although the College only looked like a hut from the outside it was not a bit like a hut inside. In the common room the walls were papered with a William Morris design wallpaper, and this theme was echoed by the curtains. The furniture was modern and tasteful. From the windows we looked across the lawn which was shielded from the road by two belts of shrubs with a very useful car park between them. In the middle of the lawn was a mulberry tree, which in season provided self-picked dessert after lunch, and once or twice a year the materials for a mulberry tart.

Lunch, in fact, soon became one of the focal points of College life, as it still is to this very day. Having dismissed an external firm of caterers within a year of the College's foundation, rather than appointing another in its place, Kits van Heyningen approached the wife of the College porter, Mr Collins, to ask whether she would take on the task of providing lunch. She agreed, and in addition to her much-anticipated mulberry tarts, Mrs Collins' skills in the kitchen were warmly appreciated by all members of the College. According to Eric Whittaker, she prepared 'good homely food, soup and a hot dish which one received from her hands at

the kitchen door, and the cold table laid out on a sideboard … but the full Stilton cheeses into which we used to dig ad lib with a tablespoon are really something to remember.' Equally memorable, it seems, were her signature dishes, 'brown onion' and 'white onion' soup, which appeared with unusual frequency on the College lunch menu. Despite their lack of culinary sophistication, these nourishing starters would later become objects of nostalgic veneration. So, too, would her home-made cheese straws, which were reserved for special occasions in the College year when drinks and snacks would be served in the Common Room following important celebrations, such as the annual thanksgiving service marking the foundation of the College, held on 25 October (St Crispin's Day), or the Carol Service towards the end of Michaelmas Term, both of which were held in St Cross Church. Although the former event would sadly disappear from the College calendar, the latter has remained an enduringly popular pre-Christmas event, in much the same way as the Founders' Feast held at the end of every Michaelmas Term.

Having left an indelible mark on the College's early history, the Collinses moved on after a few years only to be replaced by a succession of individuals who were not employed for long mainly because they could not adapt to collegiate life – or as Kits van Heyningen aptly put it later in one of his contributions to the *College Record*, simply because they 'did not really understand what was needed.' However, in February 1972, another husband-and-wife team, Mr and Mrs Helliwell, were appointed, and they not only thrived in a collegiate environment – she as the cook, he as the porter – but according to Kits were credited with being 'largely instrumental in building up the success of the College.' This was due in no small part to Mrs Helliwell's prodigious cookery skills, and throughout her twelve-years' service she not only provided some first-rate lunches but in doing so succeeded in establishing the College's reputation for the excellence of its food across the University. Despite her passion for cooking, Mrs Helliwell, it seems, also harboured other yearnings, something to which Kits teasingly alluded in his fulsome tribute to her contribution to College life following her retirement in 1984: 'She has, as far as I know, only one weakness – one that might well have tempted her to prolong her stay in the College. I am glad to think that I was able to some extent to assuage it – it is for Douglas Fairbanks, Jr.'

Mr William Helliwell, Mrs Helliwell and kitchen staff, *ca* 1975, in the kitchen of the wooden hut.

Unfortunately, very few photographs of social events at the St Cross Road site have found their way into the College archives, and so there are few visual reminders of those early days. One of the few that we have, however, catches a moment in the early 1970s when drinks were enjoyed on the lawn before members of the College and their guests retired inside to a formal dinner or feast.

Drinks on the lawn prior to a feast held in the hut, *ca* 1970.

The first graduate students

The beginning of the second academic year in the College's history marked the arrival of the first intake of graduate students. Numbering only five, each was awarded a scholarship on entry, and they were henceforth referred to by Kits van Heyningen as his 'scholars' rather than students. It was a distinction, as one student would later remark, that provided 'balm to everyone's ego.' Clearly, the lack of physical space meant that student numbers would have to be limited for the foreseeable future. In fact, the annual intake of graduate students would remain in single figures until 1981, when it rose to thirteen. Nonetheless, it was unanimously agreed that the presence of junior members would enrich College life and, perhaps more significantly, that the experience would be hugely beneficial to both fellows and students alike.

On their arrival, students were warmly welcomed into the communal life of the College, which by this stage had quickly established its own distinctive rituals and routines in the confined and – at least from our twenty-first century perspective – noxiously dense, smoke-filled atmosphere of the wooden hut.

Lunch in the hut according to Eric Whittaker in 'Recollections of a Hut Dweller':

There were a few tables lined up along the walls, each with five dining chairs – one at each end and three along one side only, because the room was not wide enough to permit chairs to be placed between the table and the wall. There were also a few low circular tables of common-room type, surrounded by easy chairs, and people also used to eat their lunch at these. Indeed the members of the College were divided into two sharply defined groups, the dining chair addicts and the easy chair addicts.

According to Jennifer Baines (at that time, Jennifer Smith), one of the first students to join the College in 1966, a major attraction of St Cross lay in the fact that it was generally perceived as being a 'grown-up' institution, unlike many traditional colleges which gave the appearance of being 'an extension of school.' Equally, at this early stage in its existence, it also offered its junior members the more intangible yet enticing prospect of 'being part of and contributing in a small way to the history of a community with the illustrious future that might be expected from an Oxford postgraduate college.' Moreover, since no Oxford experience would be complete without its black-tie gatherings and croquet on the lawn, the College's first student committee quickly ensured that St Cross would be no exception. As Roger Kitching, who also joined the College in 1966, memorably recalls, such disparate activities could occasionally coalesce, as they apparently did during one 'black-tie affair' when 'an inexhaustible supply of Pimm's generated by the good Mr Collins … concluded with croquet on the lawn at midnight – adding to the numerous handicaps of bumps, holes and mulberry tree, the additional problem of a moonless, pitch-black night.'

Five among fifty

One of the first students, Jennifer Smith (now Baines), recalls what it was like to be one of only five students among some fifty fellows:

We were spoilt rotten, welcomed and treated with warmth and generosity by the Fellowship … it was fascinating to talk with geologists, forestry experts, agriculturalists, who without exception responded to what must often have been ignorant and fatuous questions with exemplary courtesy.

Whether or not the College's celebrated egalitarian ethos could have been both engendered and sustained without such comparatively modest beginnings remains debatable. However, there can be little doubt that the continuing absence of those traditional symbols of status and hierarchy — high table and Senior Common Room — together with the sharing of College facilities by both senior and junior members alike, owes much to the communal spirit nurtured within the prefabricated walls of the wooden hut.

On-site developments

Within a matter of months after the College's foundation, Kits van Heyningen raised the prospect of installing a computer for the use of fellows and students alike – a radical idea at a time when computers were only just beginning to make their presence felt in academic life. To explore the feasibility of such an initiative in more detail, he arranged to meet one of the country's leading experts in computer technology, Sir Leon Bagrit. It soon became obvious that, given the sheer size and cost of computer hardware at the time, the College was clearly not in a position to install its own equipment. Undeterred, van Heyningen then broached his idea with Jack Howlett (later elected a fellow of the College), the Director of the Science Research Council's laboratory at Chilton, near Abingdon, who came up with a more affordable solution. At Howlett's suggestion, an agreement was reached to install a computer terminal in the College linked by a landline to the large Atlas computer network at Chilton, and thus it was that St Cross became the first Oxford College to provide its members with a remote access terminal to a computer. St Cross was not only at the forefront of computer technology in Oxford, but was also one of the first educational institutions in Europe to make use of such technology for research into the arts and humanities as well as the sciences.

Kits van Heyningen on the link to the Atlas computer network

Interviewed by reporters from the The Times on 5 April 1966, Kits van Heyningen was keen to stress what he saw as the important contribution that computers could make across all academic disciplines:

The idea began to grow on me that this was a service which could go a long way towards providing a soul for the college … The idea applies uniquely to a graduate college in Oxford because a college is a cross-section of the university and graduates have research problems to which the computer might usefully be applied.

A pressing problem, however, was where to house the computer terminal, given the absence of available space in the wooden hut. The solution was soon provided by Merton College, which agreed to the sale in September 1967 of a further strip of land on the eastern boundary of the site. This provided scope for the existing wooden building to be extended and the new computer terminal could thus be installed.

In a related on-site development, an approach was also made to the Church Authorities to enable the College to purchase a small strip of non-consecrated land on the north-west corner of the site bordering the Holy Cross (St Cross) cemetery. Once this had been agreed, the College was then able to 'square off', as it were, its small, three-quarter acre plot and thus remove a minor topographical impediment to the drawing up of plans for the new buildings. In retrospect, this might seem a modest achievement, but it was a significant early manifestation of the College's unrelenting focus on growth and development, which would ultimately enable it to transcend the limited, physical confines of its original site and expand its student numbers exponentially.

> *The College faced an unexpected objection from the poet John Betjeman to the Stout & Litchfield plans for the new buildings. ... Betjeman had played a key role in the sensitive restoration of part of the fabric of the Victorian school building and lodge after the College first occupied the St Cross Road site in 1965.*

Having successfully concluded its transaction with the Church Authorities, however, the College faced an unexpected objection from the poet John Betjeman to the Stout & Litchfield plans for the new buildings. As we have seen, Betjeman had played a key role in the sensitive restoration of part of the fabric of the Victorian school building and lodge after the College first occupied the St Cross Road site in 1965. Concerned by the planned demolition of this structure to make way for a larger, cloistered complex of modern buildings set within the quadrangular plot, Betjeman proposed a compromise which would have allowed the original Victorian building to be preserved intact and incorporated into the Stout and Litchfield design. Betjeman's proposal, had it been accepted, would have meant the sacrifice of twelve or more study bedrooms in addition to a considerable disruption to the flow of

A sketch incorporating John Betjeman's suggested revision to the original Stout & Litchfield design.

The so-called Bursars' Gate, designed by our first bursar and financed by the second bursar. It incorporates a chronogram in the inscription reading *Hanc portulam collegio sui donavit socius.*

human traffic through the site. With one disgruntled member of College rather disdainfully dismissing the proposal as an infusion of 'nostalgic charm' or a piece of 'Fantasia Betjemania', the idea was quietly dropped. Some fifty years later, however, those visitors to the new graduate accommodation jointly constructed in the mid- 1990s by St Cross and Brasenose College will see that Betjeman would ultimately have his way, for the Victorian schoolroom and lodge, which were given listed building status in 1973, are still conspicuously preserved.

Although the College would never attract sufficient funds to build a permanent home on St Cross Road, it was the grateful recipient of a number of benefactions during its foundation years. The most unusual was the so-called Bursars' Gate designed by Kenneth Knowles, our first bursar, and paid for by our second bursar, Desmond Walshaw. Knowles, who was deeply interested in the visual arts, particularly glass and wrought-iron work, incorporated a Latin chronogram in his design which reads: *Hanc portulam collegio suo donavit socius* ('A fellow gave this little gate to his College'), with a number of letters within the inscription highlighted in gold to provide, by addition of their values as Roman numerals, the following date CVLMCLLIVDVICIV, or 1973. The Bursars' Gate was originally positioned at the entrance to St Cross Church cemetery next to the Old School House but has since been removed and kept at the College's main site in St Giles where it will eventually be displayed. Knowles had also donated several pewter goblets, similarly inscribed with Latin chronograms, but his most lasting contribution to the College may well prove to be his depiction – for a car-parking permit for the St Cross Road site – of a 'cross potent' (an equal-armed cross with crossbars or 'crutches' at the four ends), since adopted as the symbolic embodiment of St Cross.

Among all the early benefactions, however, by far the most generous came from the estate of Mildred Treverton, who died in 1970. The Treverton Trust was established by her daughter Ruth van Heyningen, and through the proceeds of the Treverton Trust Kits van Heyningen was able to rekindle his personal ambition to enhance the College's new-found status through the acquisition of works of art. Before they began their search, Kits and Ruth sought the advice of two family friends, the art historian Charles Handley-Read and his wife Lavinia, a connoisseur of Victorian sculpture. Charles Handley-Read's early academic work focused on modernism and modernist architecture, but following his visit to an exhibition on 'Victorian and Edwardian Decorative Arts' at the Victoria and Albert Museum in 1952, his interests took a markedly different direction and both he and his wife became enthusiastic collectors of late nineteenth- and early twentieth-century *objets d'art*.

Under their guidance, Kits van Heyningen purchased a small number of ceramics, including a fine Hans Coper vase and an equally fine Lucie Rie bowl, together with items of glassware including several early twentieth-century pieces from the French manufacturer René Lalique and from the Lötz factory in Bohemia, as well as some contemporary (*ca* 1970) work by one of the founders of the Studio Glass Movement of Great Britain, Sam Herman. There were also a number of Art Nouveau ceramic objects, various bronze pieces and, most notably, a silvered figure entitled the 'Knight Errant' by the British sculptor, Gilbert Bayes.

Proceeds from the Trust also enabled Kits van Heyningen to commission, several years before his retirement, a portrait of himself as Master, thus allowing

OPPOSITE: Art glass (*ca* 1970) by Sam Herman. Acquired with funds from the Treverton Trust.

The Knight Errant (1898), by the British sculptor Gilbert Bayes (1872–1953). Acquired with funds from the Treverton Trust.

him to emulate a long-established tradition among Oxford Colleges. On the advice of Charles Handley-Read, he approached one of the leading artists of the day, Sir William Coldstream of the Slade School of Fine Art, who accepted the commission and set about his task with the slow deliberation and minute attention to detail that characterised his approach to portraiture. As Kits commented later in his autobiography: 'He would look at me with a ruler balanced on his finger, then with a plumbline, and make a minute mark on the canvas. Sometimes he made an invisible mark with the point of the wooden end of his brush.'

Completed after more than fifty separate sittings and considered one of the finest Oxford portraits of its time, the portrait now takes pride of place in the current College Hall alongside those of three of the four Heads of House who have so far succeeded him.

The display of a further painting by Coldstream, however, would meet with considerably less acclaim. This was a fairly large, unfinished picture entitled 'Seated Nude', which Kits purchased on behalf of the College when his own portrait was in its final stages of completion. It was never framed and was originally placed on top of one of the bookshelves in the library of Kirby Old School, which also served as a

meeting room for Governing Body. Although its elevated position may well have exerted some bearing on its critical reception, its installation in the library provoked a sense of outrage among a small number of fellows who felt it was rather too graphic for their tastes. In fact, one senior member of College felt so strongly about its presence that he resigned his fellowship. In the wake of this controversy, the 'Seated Nude' was eventually replaced by a markedly less controversial painting depicting an orange tree, about which Coldstream reputedly said that he would paint the most boring subject he could possibly think of in order to meet the tastes of the St Cross College fellowship.

The 'Seated Nude' (unfinished, 1970) by Sir William Coldstream (1908-1987). Photograph taken ca 1972 before its placement in the library of Kirby Old School.

Orange Tree, by Sir William Coldstream (1908–1987).

Migrating to '…that noble building in the heart of Oxford'

While the issue of Coldstream's female nude no doubt provoked some lively Common Room discussion about the ethical boundaries of contemporary art, debates such as this can only have provided a temporary diversion from more pressing matters of College business, in particular the College's urgent need to expand and redevelop its site. In the years leading up to Kits van Heyningen's retirement as Master of St Cross, however, an opportunity arose which could have resulted in his Coldstream portrait's hanging in a very different setting – that of a fairly substantial stone-clad building in St Aldate's, bordering Christ Church Memorial Gardens. This rather uninspiring but dignified structure, designed by Sir Hubert Worthington in 1936, had originally provided accommodation for members of St Catherine's Society, the precursor of St Catherine's College. When St Catherine's moved to its modern, purpose built complex near Holywell Manor in the early 1960s, the site was then occupied by the newly-established Linacre College before it, in turn, relocated to its current home on the northern boundary of St Cross Road, adjacent to the University Parks.

The Worthington building was initially offered by the University to St Cross in 1972 but with the proviso that the College should be prepared to offer new fellowships to what seemed like a disproportionate number of senior members of the University who still lacked any College affiliation. Despite such external pressure, the proposal to relocate was initially approved by Governing Body in April 1973. However, following a protracted debate during which the College reassessed the wisdom of such a move, the University's offer was finally rejected in January 1976.

What undoubtedly had a significant bearing on this decision was the emergence of a further initiative to redevelop the existing St Cross Road site. In fact, a provisional architect's brief for what was conceived as a 'staged development' had been drawn up as early as 1972 by Michael Brookes, University Land Agent and fellow of St Cross. Further drafts preserved in the College archives dating from 1974 include detailed proposals for new College accommodation, including a dining hall, kitchen, Common Room and offices, all of which were to be housed in the first phase of a redevelopment project that would ultimately conclude with the demolition of the wooden hut and its replacement

by a permanent structure. A sketch of the proposed building fronting St Cross Road in a 'neo-Gothic style' confirms that it was not only intended to complement the existing Victorian schoolhouse and attached lodge, but of course the church itself. In stark contrast to the earlier Stout & Litchfield proposals and while undoubtedly sympathetic to its environment, its design nonetheless seems decidedly anodyne.

Yet with an estimated cost in excess of half a million pounds, this alternative redevelopment scheme still left the College with the intractable problem of raising sufficient funds. Moreover, it leaves past and present members of St Cross with this sobering thought – that had such a substantial benefaction been forthcoming, the College would have almost certainly remained on its original site.

At the very moment when it seemed that St Cross was destined to remain in a state of financial limbo, however, the opportunity for it to share the premises of Pusey House on St Giles unexpectedly materialised. Although the prospect of either moving to the Worthington building or redeveloping the existing site had their advantages, both options were completely overshadowed by the chance to migrate to

Architectural drawings, prepared ca 1974, for proposed buildings fronting St Cross Road as part of a 'staged development' of the St Cross Road site.

a distinguished and beautifully proportioned set of buildings in the Gothic-revival style, originally designed by the architect Temple Moore at the beginning of the twentieth century and occupying an enviable position in the centre of Oxford.

How this had come about was largely a matter of happenstance. The source of the College's good fortune was Michael Brookes, whose work as University Land Agent enabled him to be among the first to hear of potential development opportunities in a city where available land was virtually non-existent. Pursuing a suggestion made to him by John Barton, also a fellow of the College, that should the Faculty of Theology (which then occupied several rooms in Pusey House) decide to relocate, St Cross could do worse than move into Pusey House, Brookes discovered that Pusey House *would* be prepared to consider sharing its premises with St Cross if suitable terms could be agreed, and he therefore lost no time in sharing such vital intelligence with Kits van Heyningen. From this point on events moved swiftly, and the College's Governing Body soon found itself examining the hugely attractive proposition of moving to an unrivalled location in the very heart of the city.

At its meeting on 10 March 1976, Governing Body voted overwhelmingly in favour of an amalgamation with Pusey House, even to the extent of endorsing a possible change of name to 'Pusey College' to acknowledge the latter's historical association with the site. Once this momentous decision had been taken, a committee including the Master and four fellows of the College – Michael Brookes, David Browning (University Lecturer in Geography), Alan Jones and Tom Tinsley (then Vice-Master of the College) – was established to negotiate the terms of the merger.

With his retirement imminent, Kits van Heyningen opted to withdraw from the negotiating committee. He was also obliged to take a back seat in an equally important affair, the election of a new Master. Since protocol demanded that this could not be discussed in Governing Body meetings in front of the existing Head of House, a committee was established to draw up a shortlist of prospective candidates. The chosen candidate was Godfrey Stafford, a distinguished scientist and head of the Rutherford Appleton Laboratory, who also had the distinction of being a Visiting Fellow of the College. He was duly elected, and as we shall see, presided over a further period of growth and consolidation in the College's new setting.

Meanwhile, negotiations with representatives of Pusey House – in which the University played a significant and generally helpful role – continued until a provisional agreement to unite both institutions under the same roof was finally reached in December, 1979. The terms of the agreement entitled the College to purchase a 999-year lease on substantial parts of Pusey House in addition to the right to develop land to the rear of the existing buildings. All that now remained was to find a solution to the financial conundrum which had preoccupied van Heyningen since the foundation of the College in 1965 – namely, how to raise the considerable sum required to complete this transaction.

The answer, however, actually lay very close at hand. It would stem, in fact, from the mutual respect and goodwill that had already developed between Kits van Heyningen and the Oxford publishers Richard Blackwell and Per Saugman. As Kits noted in his autobiography, once a provisional agreement had been reached with Pusey House, matters fell into place with remarkable rapidity. Having been invited to lunch by two fellows of St Cross – the Vice-Master Tom Tinsley and Bent Juel-Jensen – Per Saugman was duly informed of the College's ambitions to move to the Pusey House site and the sum required to facilitate this historic migration. The timing of this meeting proved fortuitous, for it happened to coincide with on-going discussions within Blackwell's about how the company could best mark its forthcoming centenary early in the New Year.

Per Saugman's recollection of events leading up to the Blackwell's benefaction, related in a memorial booklet for Richard Blackwell (d. 1980):

[Tinsley and Juel-Jensen] invited me for lunch one day, and it became quite an expensive meal, but it seemed right that Blackwell's should celebrate its centenary through its contribution to the University. Richard and I dined together that evening to discuss the suggestion and I could see him become captivated by the idea; he suddenly said 'Tell the Master he has got his college.' I rang Kits van Heyningen at midnight and apologized for the late call – and gave him the news. He said he practically fell out of the bed, for his agony as a fund-raiser was over.

Details of the Blackwell's benefaction were publicly disclosed during a special lunch to celebrate the bookstore's centenary in a chilly Merton College Hall on 3 January 1979, when Per Saugman formally presented Kits van Heyningen with the legal documentation that would enable the College not only to move from its current site on St Cross Road but, as Kits later put it, to quit the confines of a secluded wooden hut in order to occupy 'the noblest building on that noble avenue in the heart of Oxford.'

For the time being, however, Kits could savour the moment and no doubt relish the fact that his tireless quest for a substantial benefaction had, at long last, been amply rewarded. Small wonder that having delivered his acceptance speech during Blackwell's centenary lunch, he admits to experiencing a sense of euphoria, and takes to his seat once again 'feeling as fine as any man could ever hope to feel.' He could now contemplate his retirement in September of 1979 with equanimity, heartened by the knowledge that through the exceptional generosity of Blackwell's, the College's immediate future had finally been secured.

OVERLEAF: The Four Colleges Archway viewed from the west quad, St Giles site, 2010.

GROWING ON A NEW SITE
1979–1996

Diarmaid MacCulloch

As a new academic year opened in Michaelmas term 1979, decisive changes were in train for the College. A new Master faced the hard act of following a charismatic founding Head of House, and there was the ever-more-real prospect of a new site, with all the questions of identity old and new which this raised. A great deal happened in the near-decade of Godfrey Stafford's Mastership, which to those experiencing it, seemed transformational. Derek Roe (who served as Vice-Master in Godfrey's later years in office) summarised this sea-change, speaking at the memorial service for Godfrey in 2013: 'Stafford inherited a College with only a handful of graduate students, still housed in a wooden hut, still critically short of funds, and still uncertain of what its aspirations were, let alone of how it could possibly realise them. When he retired in the autumn of 1987, the move to St Giles had been made, numbers of students were at last able to increase, plans for a new wing had been completed, and the first substantial benefactions had been received.'

It is true that the first great gift was in place during the last year of Kits' Mastership, in that presentation from Blackwell's at the chilly lunch in Merton Hall; yet the knowledge of secure funding for the next step is good cheer for any Master-Elect. Godfrey would be conscious that his time was going to be much stretched both in timetable and location, for he came to St Cross as a part-time Master, continuing with his hugely important work as a particle physicist and director of the Rutherford Appleton Laboratory at Harwell, ten miles south of Oxford.

The armillary sphere sundial, a memorial to Ronald Hurst, the College's oldest graduate student so far, given by his family. Garden of west quad on the St Giles site, 2013.

In 1981, Godfrey gave up his Directorship of the Laboratory to devote fuller attention to the College, but he never ceased to be a working scientist at the very highest level.

And so a cheerfully eventful Michaelmas Term 1979 ensued. On 4 December 1979 the Governors of Pusey House unanimously approved legal documents, followed a week afterwards by the Governing Body of St Cross, creating the 999-year lease, still in place (with minor adjustments). Godfrey could commemorate these milestones a day or two later at the Founders' Feast, taking the opportunity to establish a pardonable break with tradition in making a speech to celebrate what he referred to as 'the merger', a formulation that subsequent tensions rendered a little optimistic. This Feast might itself be seen as a little gesture of self-assertion amid collegiate Oxford: no booking in one of the grand halls or dining-rooms of the older Colleges had proved possible amid the crowded Christmas calendar, so St Cross proudly toasted its new prospects in the cosy setting of its own hut.

Aerial view showing the Pusey House site as it appeared at the time of the agreement with St Cross.

RIGHT: Detail of the St Giles area from the map published in 1675 by David Loggan, *Nova & Accuratissima Celeberrimae Universitatis Civitatisque Oxoniensis Scenographia.* The present location of St Cross College is marked out in red.

LEFT: Detail from the Ordnance Survey map of 1876 showing the St Giles area. The present location of St Cross College is indicated in red.

Preparations for the move

There could be no imminent move, for a huge amount must now be done on the St Giles site to prepare it for its new joint role (and it was sad that just after this year ended came the death in 1980 of Richard Blackwell, the benefactor who had made it all possible, yet who did not have the chance to see the result of his generosity). The quality of the buildings was such that they demanded an even more imaginative response than Kits van Heyningen had brought to the task of creating a memorable interior in a featureless wooden hut. Pusey House, a commemoration of the prominent Anglo-Catholic divine Edward Bouverie Pusey (1800–1882) and incorporating his magnificent library, was a foundation of 1884. It originally occupied 61 St Giles, one house among the ranks of 'burgage' properties that lined the Anglo-Norman commercial development of St Giles north of the Anglo-Saxon town of Oxford. Each house stood (or stands) at the front of a long strip of garden or open space backing on a common stone boundary wall, whose origins are as old as the Normans, and which on our side of St Giles, still retains much of its monumental quality in those lengths that survive.

Gradually Pusey House bought adjacent properties and in 1911 began an ambitious plan of rebuilding, to create an ensemble which would indeed be worthy of housing an Oxford College, and which includes the entire present precinct of St Cross College's central site. The architect was Temple Moore, a favourite among Anglo-Catholic patrons, and one of the most distinguished exponents of the Gothic style: the result was both robust and exquisite in detail. One engaging feature of Moore's design was that he saved some of the fine internal features of the Georgian houses which were demolished and reused them to create some delightful domestic interiors in a contrasting style to the free Perpendicular Gothic which gave the House's buildings their outward unity. Thus Pusey House exhibits a stylistic 'unity by inclusivity', a favourite principle of a succeeding and equally distinguished architect, Sir Ninian Comper, who later designed some superb fittings and stained glass for the *pièce de resistance* of Temple Moore's buildings, the great two-hall chapel of the House.

Now, life in the hut had a new preoccupation, as Master, fellows and students considered the ways in which their life was about to change and engender a more elaborate infrastructure. They launched the *St Cross College Record*, which over the next few years would

Pusey Quad looking east, at the time of the agreement with St Cross.

Pusey House before St Cross

The late Dr Brian Atkins (opposite), emeritus fellow and a member of the Working Party that negotiated with the fellows of Pusey House, could reminisce about the House much further back than the foundation of the College or the merger, since in 1955 he had been a guest for a week there thanks to his former school chaplain Fr Philip Curtis (from Giggleswick School in Yorkshire), who had become Pusey House Librarian. Brian remembers:

at breakfast there were as many as six clergymen, several of whom must have been temporary visitors. The most conspicuous of these was a bishop who, each morning, would prop against the marmalade jar the tabloid paper of the day, which he studied avidly. It was explained to me that this was 'in order to see how the other half lives, dear boy.' I remember best a return bus journey on a glorious summer's day above the Windrush Valley, Philip bearing bags of his laundry being processed for him by a community of nuns at Burford.

provide a lively and fascinating chronicle of the College's expanding life, much enriched by diverse academic wit generally within the bounds of political tact. In the first issue at the end of this 1979–80 year, the then Senior Tutor Godfrey Tyler reported that alongside the sixty-six current fellows, there were fourteen students in residence, of whom eight were women. 'With the expected move to the Pusey site … it should eventually be possible to give effect to the College's long expressed wish for a greatly expanded student body', he commented, naturally following this with an appeal for funds.

One essential consideration for an Oxford College must be its heraldry. Before any readers sneer at such a piece of medieval flummery, they should consider a coat of arms' role as a corporate logo: think how many hours and pots of money commercial corporations pour into such symbols. And so the first discussions opened about what to do for a coat of arms, involving John Tiffany and Paul Morgan, two members of the College learned in such matters, who were appointed the

College Sub-Committee for Heraldic Affairs. Their no doubt enjoyable ruminations involved Mr Michael Maclagan, who was then both Richmond Herald and long-term Tutor in History at Trinity College. The response of the University Registrar was discouraging: 'Since St Cross College has the status of a University Department, we cannot allow it to apply for a grant of arms; to do so might well open the floodgates, with Biochemistry or Music kitting themselves out with appropriately symbolic escutcheons.' The Registrar advised waiting for independence. The Committee duly desisted, officially at least, though John's creative imagination continued to ferment. As late as 1988 Governing Body was to accept his eventual ingenious design for the coat of arms (which after much tergiversation over the decades, fixed the exact nature of the cross after which the College is named), and the notorious dilatoriness of the College of Arms further postponed the formal grant of the coat till the late 1990s.

Prospects for the future

At the end of the academic year, on 21 June 1980, Pusey House and St Cross College met together on the St Giles site in Pusey Chapel, where the Pusey clergy brought their accustomed Anglo-Catholic splendour to celebrating a Eucharist of the Holy Spirit. Principal Cheslyn Jones preached on the adroitly appropriate text of Genesis 2.18 (which precedes God's creation of Eve from Adam's rib), 'It is not good for man to be alone', admitting as a celibate that 'I have never found myself using this text before, and I have never taken its most obvious advice.' His sermon intriguingly paid tribute to 'a casual remark of John Barton' (College Chaplain and Fellow in Theology) as the origin of the whole St Cross/Pusey scheme, and he significantly remarked how many fellows of St Cross were members of the Oriental Institute next door to the House. This had relevance to plans which loomed large for the next two decades as one possible major strand in the College's life: 'Associated' study centres which concentrated on the culture and traditions of the three 'Abrahamic' faiths, Christianity, Judaism and Islam. There was already an association between the College and the Oxford Centre for Hebrew and Jewish Studies (founded in 1972 as the Oxford Centre for

Postgraduate Hebrew Studies, with the College founding fellow David Patterson at its head), and it was around this time that the possibility of a Centre for Islamic Studies associated with the University was first being discussed, as we will see.

Only a fortnight later, on 1 July 1980, the University finally signed the 999 year lease on behalf of the College. It was a moment of harmony and optimism well symbolised the following day at the official handover in a set-piece photograph at the principal entrance on St Giles. In this picture, Principal Cheslyn Jones and his colleague Canon Gareth (Garry) Bennett warmly shake hands with Master Godfrey Stafford and Vice-Master Eric Whittaker. Flanking them (outside the photo) are new nameboards for the two institutions, identical in size and design: a mark of good intentions for the future. Before St Cross College arrived, it had always been the practice of Pusey House to advertise its activities by the front door, naturally enough, and the College did not want to interfere with that. So Eric Whittaker designed two name boards, one for the College and one for Pusey, which were carved in hardwood, and put them up at the two sides of the front door. Wonderfully resilient in the face of Oxford weather and traffic fumes, they still grace the entrance today.

2 July 1980: the two parties shake hands at the St Giles entrance. *Left to right*: Canon Gareth Bennett, Canon Cheslyn Jones (Principal of Pusey House), Godfrey Stafford (Master of St Cross College), Eric Whittaker (Vice-Master).

What would the new agreements mean in practical terms? There was much goodwill for both institutions to develop their activities on the joint site and take new directions. Behind the handsome Gothic Revival quad created by Temple Moore and his successors, there was a walled-in garden providing open space almost unrivalled in potential in central Oxford; it cried out for development that Pusey had never been financially able to pursue. One possibility was a purpose-built building for the Pusey House Library (which also in that era doubled as the University's Theology Faculty Library): the idea in this scheme, as the Master was still proposing in his Founders' Feast speech of November 1981, was that the stately interior of the present Pusey Library would become a Common Room, presumably for both institutions.

Anticipating this or similar agreements, the College bought the late Georgian property of 1 Beaumont Buildings just off St John Street, to provide three self-contained flats for the Pusey Chapter, with one more envisaged. The College further strengthened the institutional link by creating three Pusey Fellowships for clergy of the House, with full voting rights on the Governing Body (it was a shame that Cheslyn Jones, who had been in office throughout the negotiations for the new site, retired at the end of this academic year, before there was a chance for him to become a fellow of the College under the agreement of 1980). At this stage, Pusey House was so willing to envisage a sharing of activities that it reciprocally elected two fellows of St Cross on to its Board of Governors, one of them John Barton the Chaplain, the other Eric Whittaker the Vice-Master; John and Eric took part in the choice of the next Principal of the House, the Rev. Philip Ursell. This made sense, if Pusey House were more formally to develop its academic activities. A Pusey Centre for Christian Studies was planned and could soon be seen as one possible completion for the three Associated 'Abrahamic' study centres alongside the Oxford Centre for Hebrew and Jewish Studies and the embryonic Oxford Centre for Islamic Studies.

> *At this stage, Pusey House was so willing to envisage a sharing of activities that it reciprocally elected two fellows of St Cross on to its Board of Governors, one of them John Barton the Chaplain, the other Eric Whittaker the Vice-Master.*

A new College life begins

Pusey House Chapel, naturally enough given these prospects, began to play a part in the life of the College. It now became the setting for the annual College St Crispin's Day service customarily held in late October, and it also hosted the College carol service (instituted not long before the prospect of the new site opened up), adorned by a choir under the direction of Donald Richards and Jim Williamson. Yet the pleasantly villagey atmosphere of St Cross parish church made it an attractive alternative venue in 1980 for one of the first College weddings. One of the then scholars, Jane Whitehead (now Gaskell), married in St Cross Church, followed by a reception next door in the College hut. John Barton officiated as College chaplain, the solemnly-constituted *Cantores Sanctae Crucis* provided the choir, while a former scholar in music played the organ. Only the bell-ringers (and the bridegroom) had to be recruited from beyond the College.

Student intake for 1980–81 increased in anticipation of the new site – an overall total of no fewer than seventeen students in residence for this academic year, nine of them women. This was the first year that the College introduced a system of senior sponsors, which still endures, though it has a rather different dynamic now that the ratio

27 March 1982: the wedding of David Andrews, Senior Research Fellow, to a College Scholar, Kathleen Daly, in the Catholic Chaplaincy, with the reception in the Saugman Hall. This was the first completely College wedding – the College choir, of which they were both members, provided the music. *Left to right:* Desmond Walshaw (Best Man, a fellow of St Cross), Colin Andrews (David's brother), Margaret Andrews (David's mother), David Andrews, Kathleen Daly, Sheila and Patrick Daly (Kathleen's parents), Hélène La Rue (Bridesmaid, later to become a fellow of St Cross).

of fellows to students has so dramatically reversed. It was not until 1987, on the proposal of the junior members, that first College officers and later all sponsors began taking on a systematic responsibility for graduate 'collections', known today as graduate consultations. It is an interesting sign of persistent College informality that up till that date, collections had not been thought necessary. Another inauguration of a College tradition came at this time with the first College seminar, given by David G. Andrews, Senior Research Fellow (and later Professor of Physics) on the topic of atmospheric waves. This was the first of several given by new fellows explaining their work. It is a tradition that has waxed and waned, one of the first wanings being as early as the mid-1980s!

Still in an exhilarating era of firsts, March 1981 saw the beginning of office for the College's first Proctor, Robert (Bob) E. White, who was elected Junior Proctor after 'a close-fought contest' between several candidates from among the fellowship who were eligible under the rather exacting rules. Bob later became Professor of Soil Science at the University of Melbourne. He nominated College fellows Tom Hassall and George Smith as Pro-Proctors. Given the majestically slow pace of the Proctorial cycle, the next such opportunity was not to appear again until March 1993, when the College's second Proctor and first Senior Proctor, Philip Allen, was installed. He chose as his Pro-Proctors Brian Woolnough and Nick Kruger. Rather more exotic in its lack of precedent was a ceremony at Oxford's Maison Française on 25 November 1980, when the fellowship could bask in Kits van Heyningen's reflected glory as a *Chevalier de l'Ordre National du Mérite*, for his services to microbiology and bacteriology, and his warm personal links with France.

At the Founders' Feast on 11 December 1980, Godfrey Stafford was able to note that it was almost certainly the last to be held on the old site, also ruefully reflecting that 'a large single benefaction, such as Green College in Oxford and Robinson College in Cambridge have been successful in attracting, still evades us.' The significance of these examples was that the respective donors had provided so much money that the Colleges took their names. With a move from a site in St Cross Road to one with no such organic associations with the name St Cross, it was a moment to be thinking afresh about such a renaming of our own

OPPOSITE ABOVE:
The cloister on the
south side of the
Pusey Quad before
remodelling.

OPPOSITE BELOW:
The new Hall after
incorporation of the
cloister, 1981.

College, and it has remained a lurking thought ever since. But for the moment, far from a lurking thought was the monumental building work in the St Giles site, solving the problem of how those parts of it available to the College could best be put to a new use. Here, the intervention of Godfrey Stafford was crucial, as Eric Whittaker recalls:

> 'When we first moved in it was by no means obvious how we would use the buildings. What is now the library had been Pusey [House]'s dining room, served by a hatch from the kitchen that was at the east end of what is now the Saugman Common Room. This was very inadequate for our needs, but I suggested that we should initially use this for lunch, supplemented by tables in the circulation space outside the dining room door. Fortunately the Master had a much better vision and designed a steel reinforced ceiling to what is now the Saugman Room sufficiently strong to support the walls of the first floor, and permit the removal of load-bearing walls that divided up the ground floor ... Thus we were provided with a dining hall.'

Godfrey's bold scheme (so bold that the principal girder for the new ceiling had to be lifted over the top of the quad before being manoeuvred into position) had made possible this transformation from an open cloister backed by a series of nondescript small rooms to one in which the cloister arches became the beautiful sequence of Common Room windows which open northwards on to the quad.

A time of firsts

The new dining Hall which emerged from Godfrey's plans contained recessed illuminated display cases for the Mildred Treverton Trust Collection of pottery and glass, provided by the Trust administered by the first Master and his wife Ruth (a founding fellow). Already there were water-colours on loan from the marvellous collection built up by Professor Geoffrey and Mrs Audrey Blackman. The recently-widowed Mrs Blackman also gave framed *University Almanack*s; one of these is an exceptionally pretty picture of the Kirby Old School, which amid the *Almanack*'s venerable series of University and College views, had helped publicise the existence of St Cross in its early years. The Treverton Trust paid for the tables and chairs in the Hall; these are still the nucleus of the present Hall's furniture, proving their fine quality over so far more than three decades. The chairs were specially designed by Simon Porter (Bursar for a decade from 1977) and made by Crowdys, formerly of Clanfield, now based in Faringdon, who soon affectionately knew it

ST. CROSS COLLEGE, KIRBY OLD SCHOOL.

From a drawing by Birkin Haward

The Kirby Old School at the St Cross Road site, from a drawing by Birkin Haward, rendered in colour in the *Oxford Almanack* of 1977.

OPPOSITE: A vase by Hans Coper (1920–1981), purchased with funds from the Treverton Trust.

simply as 'the St Cross Chair.' The van Heyningens went on to make donations which created the display cases in the present Library room.

Not neglecting the College's face onto the world, the Treverton Trust also funded the cleaning of the stonework to the façade on St Giles, like all Oxford limestone blackened by decades of pollution. The exteriors inside the quad as yet remained dirty, but by November 1981, the Pilgrim Trust would agree to pay for this (no doubt through the advocacy of the College's honorary fellow, the great antiquary and philanthropist Marc Fitch), and that project started in March 1982. Two public rooms in the St Giles façade (eastern) wing remained shared by the College and Pusey House: the Frederic Hood Room and the Van Heyningen Room (which was at that stage a name designating a handsome panelled room on the first floor, now transferred to describe an intimate College dining room below it). There was a Common Room and bar in the east basement, which still needed a name, but never got one. Three different areas in the basement, with even smaller outposts around them, provided for the first time what could pass for a wine cellar. For a decade after 1981, this remained the shape for the College's life.

> September 1981 saw the grand opening ceremonies for all this. The new buildings witnessed a record number of students: twenty-seven in residence, seven of them actually living on site.

September 1981 saw the grand opening ceremonies for all this. The new buildings witnessed a record number of students: twenty-seven in residence, seven of them actually living on site. The students, reported John Barton as Senior Tutor, were adamant that there should be no separation into Senior and Junior Common Rooms, 'regarding ourselves as a single community so far as is possible', though John noted that 'it is not an easy position to hold in Oxford.' The following year, the number reached a statutory upper limit then imposed on the College by the University: thirty-six. They were given a representative place on the Executive Committee and the Governing Body, and the number of students necessitated electing officers with specific portfolios: secretary, bar 'liaison' and sporting and social activities. Godfrey Tyler, as retiring President of Common Room (an office formally created in 1983), emphatically restated his belief in the lack of separation when writing in

College Wine In Earlier Days

Philip Beckett, sometime College wine steward, reminisces for the 1994 College Record. *It is reassuring to note that in his time, one of the College doctors, Dr Michael Kenworthy-Browne, served on the Wine Committee. Philip recalls that when various areas of the new building became available for wine storage:*

access to some of these areas was not easy, and the annual audit could be like an obstacle race. Happily, this space became available in time for the golden years of '82 and '83 claret. So Sonia Hawkes and Simon Porter made extensive purchases. (I took over Simon's classification of 'VVIP', 'VIP', Feast and Dinner wines). They also sold the residue of the 1970 claret. Most of the 'long lifers' among their purchases were stored in the Chapel cellar where they matured in a quiet, alcoholic ambience like elderly fellows, free of the challenges of a varying environment. We are still drinking these, and the '85s and '86s that Simon bought. … On Simon's departure the cellar moved under less certain control (John Dickson's and my own). It became necessary to formalise procedures in order to strengthen inexperience by continuity. By the time this was achieved the cellar had become rather unbalanced. The good clarets at the top were no longer supported by sufficient of the less glorious reds, and there were few whites.

White wines are more difficult to manage than red, since only a few of those we can afford will endure or benefit from long storage, and many of them must be drunk young. So turnover is quite fast and, unlike the reds, one may not have a buffer of wines that one had not planned to begin until next year, but which could be drunk now if necessary. … By 1993 the residue of the '55 ports needed professionally re-corking. Also we can hardly afford to drink port at (now) about £30 a bottle. So these have been sold. We should be alright now. Now that it is in balance the cellar must be self-supporting. I keep a running total of the value of wines sold to College members and to outside bodies holding dinners in College, and of the notional values of wine drunk on College occasions. Taking one term with another the running total of the costs of wine that we purchase must not exceed this running total of consumption.

Furniture made by Crowdys, in the 'new' Hall in the South Wing opened in 1993.

the *College Record* in 1986: 'it fosters the friendly and informal relations between junior and senior members which is one of the great strengths of St Cross. Long may it remain so.' Peter Mackridge, his successor, echoed him in 1988, and the College has stuck to this founding principle.

Glimpses of the early life of this Common Room remain, some of them reminiscent of an older Oxford. A Wager Book was instituted, Common Room President Tyler winning a pint of claret with one of the three first wagers laid. Among issues debated was 'the emotive question of smoking in the Common Room', a matter not finally settled throughout the College premises until the beginning of the twenty-first century. The first junior members' report in the *College Record* (1983) was jointly written by Alan Grainger (now in the School of Geography at Leeds) and Sally Mapstone. Sally has gone on to be a Pro-Vice-Chancellor of the University – might her governance skills exhibited in later life have something to do with this sudden flurry of organisation, including the organisation of a regular newsletter for students? It is at this time that we first hear of the 'Scottish Supper' still so popular in a more accurate designation as Burns Night Hall, and in June 1983 came the first of the College barbecues, in which Jim Williamson then and long after had a hand – though our benefactor Audrey Blackman was also energetic in preparing strawberries and chopping cucumber.

Not surprisingly, sporting activities followed. Co-operation with Wolfson College Rowing Club began, and has never ceased. In Hilary Term 1984, the College won its first football match, and in Trinity Term 1984 played its first cricket match, against Jesus College, losing by four wickets: Junior Research Fellow Farhan Nizami, the *College Record* noted, was 'discovered as the College all-rounder.' On 2 December 1990 the College's first Rugby Blue, Mark Egan, was selected for the Oxford team announced at Vincent's Club, Oxford, and within the next fortnight, Oxford had won against Cambridge in the Varsity Match.

The College has twice been in the vanguard of sporting innovation in Oxford, first with ice-hockey, thanks to its contingent of Canadian students. In 1992 James Robertson and friends from his Biochemistry Lab started hiring the Oxford ice-rink to play for fun, recruiting St Cross friends to make up numbers. 'Midnight practices every couple of weeks became a St Cross event' reminisces one of their number, Christine Schams. Good fruit came of it on 10 November 1993, when the College won the University Ice Hockey Cuppers, and naturally two Canadians were among the players. Soon after this triumph came a second momentous sporting event: on 29 October 1994, the College hosted the World Tiddlywinks Championship, after domestic enthusiasm generated by the presence in the student body of the ex-world champion Andy Purvis (Andy's other subject was the comparative biology of primate evolution, and he is at present Professor of Biodiversity at Imperial College, London). Subsequent achievements on all sporting fronts are too numerous to list.

The rehoused College led collegiate Oxford in an important respect right from the moment that it arrived in St Giles in 1981: it appointed a Director of Computing, Susan Hockey, and boasted a computer line with a VT55 terminal made available to the College by a gift of one of the computer manufacturers. Susan spoke proudly in the 1982 *College Record* of 'a modern visual display screen and keyboard which is connected to the Computing Service via a private telephone line which the College will rent from the GPO.' All this, installed in late October 1981, replaced the even more pioneering equipment which the College had possessed since soon after its foundation, and which was now little used as it was obsolete. Now College members, via the Rutherford Library, would have a route into 'the Oxford Gandalf', so that they would 'be able to search the serials catalogue from the College instead of visiting the Library to do so.' There were computer classes for College members in Hilary Term 1982 and two fellows had specialisms in computing subjects, Bill Clocksin and Tim Clement. The gradual march of computing could be discerned in the fact that this same issue of the *College Record* was the first to be typeset on the 'Lasercomp phototypesetter' at the University Computing Service.

12 November 1981 witnessed a grand celebration dinner graced by a speech from Harold Macmillan, in the presence of the Vice-Chancellor and many Heads of House. No record is preserved of its content, but the Master (speaking at a Founders' Feast judiciously postponed to March 1982), asserted bravely that 'the memory of [his

On 29 October 1994, the College hosted the World Tiddlywinks Championship, after domestic enthusiasm generated by the presence in the student body of the ex-world champion Andy Purvis.

words] will remain with those who were privileged to be present for a long time to come.' It was the occasion for the complete consumption of the batch of Burgundy bought with forethought in the late 1960s for just such an occasion, and it more or less put an end to the 1955 Croft's and Cockburn's vintage port bought around 1966.

What also became painfully apparent that evening in 1981, in a recollection for the 1994 *College Record* by the College wine steward Philip Beckett, was the appalling acoustic of the Hall, something which was partially remedied later with work to its ceiling. Crowding, too, rapidly became obvious at these major feasts, coupled with the fact that the only room for gatherings before dinner was the adjacent Lange Common Room, delightful, but too small, and in reaction to

College Life In The 1980s

Alumnus Brent Jenkins (DPhil Metallurgy, 1985) remembers St Cross College in the 80s:

It was with great anticipation that I had planned to visit St Cross College during a business trip in October 2012. It was 24 years since I graduated with a DPhil; it was clear that the College had grown significantly since 1985, when I knocked on the front door of the College to start my graduate studies. January was an odd time to arrive, which I realised when I was met by an almost empty College and deserted laboratory. I was shown to my room on the top floor of the original College building: luckily I left my cat behind as I would not have been able to swing it in that room! I was not surprised to see that the room is now used as an office/ broom cupboard. As the rest of my fellow residents returned from their festive season break and life at the College began to rekindle, I felt more at home. The residents of the original College building were actually very nice and we quickly became friends. We were also drivers of a number of College events and activities: video nights in the bar, punting, sunbathing in the back of the College (frowned upon), the College choir and various evening events ensued. On one particular evening I was introduced to a Long Island Iced Tea by one American student that really had an impact – especially that night and the next day!

The College was growing fast at that time and I was joined by two other Australians and it was nice to have some company from down-under. However, one of these Australians suffered some major injuries when he fell from the top floor of the original College building after trying to climb into his room. I clearly remember visiting him in hospital and him hobbling around during his rehabilitation.

these problems, plans were quickly made for the present dining Hall. Catering, whether for the daily weekday lunch or for greater dinners, was now on a much greater scale than in former years. It was indeed the end of an era when in June 1984, Mrs Helliwell, widow of the former College steward William Helliwell, retired after a dozen years as College Housekeeper, catering having been the major part of her empire. Kits van Heyningen in an affectionate eulogy for the *College Record*, commented that 'although Mrs Helliwell is a dear old friend of mine, of many of us, I do not know her first name … I wouldn't dream of asking her what it is, and if I did know it, I wouldn't dare use it; and when she wrote me a note recently, she signed it "Mrs H." That is her cool style and I love her for it.'

Portrait of Per Saugman by Mrs F de Rohan Wilner (professional name Vesla Stranger) painted in 1975.

The Hall had been appropriately named in honour of Per Saugman, the name it retains as our present Common Room, and there were other donors who in the next year were thanked in a rather more subtle way. Those looking at the three arches leading between our two quads will notice four shields which to the heraldically literate announce four major collegiate benefactors (All Souls, Christ Church, Merton, St. John's). So officially this thoroughfare is the Four Colleges Arch. On 7 June 1983 (one of the few sunny days that month – more recent St Crossers, take heart), there was a ceremony in what was now formally renamed the Richard Blackwell Quad, at which Sir Basil Blackwell unveiled the plaque commemorating the family benefaction. It was another milestone in creating the

7 June 1983:
Sir Basil Blackwell
unveils the plaque
commemorating the
Blackwell's benefaction,
applauded by the
Master, Godfrey
Stafford.

BELOW: Autumn 1988:
a College reading
party led by John
Barton (3rd from
right) at St Deiniol's
Library, Hawarden.

ensemble of buildings and features so familiar to later members of the College. The ambitious alterations to the quad and College interiors had quite rightly won an Oxford Preservation Trust Environmental award.

On 1 April 1982, Rev. Philip Ursell, previously Assistant Chaplain in the University of Wales and then Chaplain of Emmanuel College, Cambridge, had become Principal of Pusey House. In his installation sermon on 1 May, he said 'Pusey House is at the beginning of a happy relationship with a new College', and that year, he would prepare one member of the College for Anglican confirmation. At this stage, the Chapel was increasingly used by St Cross, with the College choir hoping 'to provide the College with more frequent choral services in the future' and already joining in Pusey House services for Corpus Christi and an Evensong in Trinity Term. There were lunchtime College prayers on Wednesdays at 1.00, occasionally with the choir providing a short anthem; these continued into 1983. Later there were regular eucharists in the Van Heyningen Room, and in 1987, a joint retreat in Surrey with people from Nuffield College. Services continued in Pusey House chapel, including an Eastertide service featuring the College choir, right up to 1991. John Barton moved in 1991 to be Oriel and Laing Professor of the Interpretation of Holy Scripture, and the College did not appoint a successor as Chaplain, though in the early 1990s Fr Michael R. Knight, one of the Pusey Fellows, did much to fill that role while he was still at Pusey House.

Study Centres and the College

In these years, the idea of three Centres of Abrahamic religions closely associated with St Cross still seemed a major possibility for the future. One element of the three must be Islam. David Browning, a fellow since three years after the College's foundation, University Lecturer in Geography, and without whom the present flourishing state of the Oxford Centre for Islamic Studies on the eastern skyline of the University is inconceivable, remembers that his association came in 1981 through an invitation to him from a group of Muslim students to be the senior member of a new University Islamic Society: that link came through his personal contacts with a former student from Saudi

Arabia. David remembers the idea of the Centre as then emerging from a conversation with Farhan Nizami in 1982, and taking its inspiration from the way that the Centre for Hebrew and Jewish Studies had been set up and expanded. So it was not 'the results of specific conditions attached to a major benefaction' but 'the results of a conversation between a Muslim and a Christian who, together, sought to follow the teachings of their respective faiths.' Between 21 and 24 July 1983, David hosted in the College an initial meeting with leading figures from a number of Asian and Arab academic institutions, to define the aims and purpose of an Oxford Centre for Islamic Studies.

In October 1985 the founding trustees of the Centre met in St Cross, and a year later came agreement from the University Council that it should formally be associated with the University, via a link with St Cross. So Miles Blackwell (a supernumerary fellow of the College) represented the College on the Board of Trustees and St Cross elected the Centre's director, Farhan Nizami (a former Junior Research Fellow), to a fellowship, with three visiting academics elected to visiting fellowships. Centre lectures and seminars were held at St Cross, and an arrangement with St Cross allowed the Centre to lease the now redundant wooden hut as its home, an occupation which endured till autumn 1994. In June 1988, David Browning took early retirement from Geography in order to devote his time fully to the Centre as it moved to the hut, and the College elected him to a Fellowship by Special Election to continue the association. Nevertheless a prophetic hint of things to come, and of the present realignment of the Centre elsewhere, was the fact that in 1985 the President of Magdalen College was the University Council's first representative on the Board of Trustees of the Centre.

In a parallel initiative for Christianity, in 1984 the well-known theologian, Arthur Peacocke, began the establishment of the Ian Ramsey Centre in two rooms of the College. This was a memorial to a brilliant but tragically workaholic Bishop of Durham, who before his early death in 1972 had strongly advocated a Christian centre which would bring together the study of ethics, science and religion. In the absence of any progress on a Pusey study centre, this could represent the Christian element in a trio of centres, alongside the nascent Islamic Centre and the Hebrew Centre already flourishing in its fine manor house out at Yarnton (which in September 2014 it left to take up accommodation in Walton

A St Cross Latin Sermon

On 15 January 1984, Peter Glare (a fellow of St Cross and editor of the *Oxford Latin Dictionary*) preached the University Latin Sermon in the University Church, one of the few fellows even then who could have done this. Here is a taster: *Hoc profecto habemus ubique praesens signum fidei nostrae. quid ergo? in crucis uestrae nomine (dixerit fortasse quispiam) quae scelera non admissa sunt? nonne hic aduersarium in custodiam ad tortores ad carnificem remittit? non uicinum ille flammifera sublata cruce trucidat? certe. non alii cruce in terram alienam defixa sub praetextu pacis seruitutem inferunt? non caeca peruicacia bellum gerunt? non negamus. sicut enim Deum nostra imagine fingere temptamus, ita crucem per quam saluationem mundo intulet ad nostrum exemplar et in nostram gloriam fabricamus.*

   'We have then an omnipresent symbol of our faith. What then? Someone will claim that every sort of crime has been committed in the name of the cross; that one man had consigned his adversary to prison, torture and execution; that another holding aloft a flaming cross has slaughtered his neighbour. True. He will say that others have planted the cross on foreign soil and imposed slavery under pretext of peace; that they fight wars with blind obstinacy. This is not to be denied. For just as we try to make God in our image, so do we construct the cross by which he brought salvation to the world according to our own pattern and for our glory.'

Peter Glare finding inspiration in the College bar, 1982.

Street in central Oxford). Formally inaugurated on 22 February 1985, the Ramsey Centre had an inauguration dinner at St Cross with the Bishop's widow as guest of honour. Peacocke (who was elected an 'Ian Ramsey Fellow' of the College, echoing the earlier institution of Pusey Fellows) was the Centre's first director, and its second was Caroline Miles, benefactor of the College, after whom a room has been named. Like the Oxford Centre for Islamic Studies, the Ramsey Centre, although now revived and very active in the Faculty of Theology and Religion following a relaunch in the last decade, is no longer closely related to the College in institutional terms. It is perhaps appropriate that the three Centres' growth has been organic and not following any one strategic path. David Browning always emphasises that none of them were created or sustained by the University but were conceived and developed by a group of individuals from within and beyond Oxford. As he rightly remarks, that was how Colleges started as well (though our history shows that St Cross and Wolfson have been the exceptions to that rule).

Money again

With substantial buildings as a visible sign of a new era from the early 1980s, a trickle of funds began to underpin the growing life of St Cross. 1983 saw a gift from the trusts of Sir Edward Abraham whose income would be used first to support the work of (now Honorary) Fellow David Warrell in Tropical Medicine, but then for a research scholarship or fellowship: this was one of the first of such donations for the College, and they still happily continue to grow in number. The University was now capitalising the annual income grant from the common College contribution, so there was a possibility of building up a proper endowment, the first step towards independence for the College, eighteen years after the foundation. Pledges from donors in this year reached a sum unprecedented in all the hard years of seeking outside generosity: four hundred thousand pounds. All this encouraged the launch of a major fundraising campaign for a new library (still at first envisaged as a joint creation with Pusey House) and a new, more adequate dining hall. It was designed to run for two years and sought a million pounds for building and a million

St Cross: an archaeological perspective

At the farewell dinner for Master Godfrey Stafford on 30 September 1987, Derek Roe went into archaeological mode: I can't resist a brief speculation as to how future archaeologists might see the same events, based doubtless on excavation. The College's first site was a light and simple rectangular structure of wood, not far from a river, and separated only by a single wall from wild country where deer roamed. The inhabitants presumably lived on hunted meat, and fish, and also apparently on mulberries; that this diet did them no good is clear from the very large adjacent cemetery. The St Giles site however is stone built, right in a city centre, and rich in art objects. We can say little of the inhabitants' diet and life span except that there were twice as many mulberry trees and no cemetery at all: perhaps the Fellows ate each other. In Stage 3 there will be greatly expanded buildings and only a tiny mulberry tree, but I won't peer further ahead.

for endowment. Consonant with this fundraising drive, a St Cross College Association had its first AGM in 1984, declaring its total membership as standing at 196.

Accordingly in 1984 preliminary plans began for a first building on the garden site behind Temple Moore's existing quad, to form the southern part of the new quadrangle, containing dining hall, kitchen and study-bedrooms. The idea of a joint library building with Pusey House had quickly ceased to form part of this scheme (and indeed, the Faculty of Theology Library found its own premises elsewhere in the next few years). There was half a million pounds in hand for the building, and it was hoped to begin building in 1986 – hopes which were to be dashed by the slow pace of the planning process with the City Council (beginning with a blank refusal without discussion from the City planning committee – not the last time the College was to have such an experience). Money was not now lacking: a large benefaction from Mr C. Ian Skipper came in 1987, together with other

gifts from Mr Samuel J. Lefrak and Mrs Caroline Enders. There was also unobtrusive and much-appreciated help from the University in making available houses in Wellington Square to provide the College with a Master's Lodge and some student accommodation, at a time when it would have been impossible for St Cross to buy property for itself in the property market of the time.

Godfrey Stafford was thus cheated of the chance to launch yet another building scheme before his long and happy retirement in North Hinksey with Goldy his wife, at the end of the academic year 1986–7. The conclusion of his Mastership was marked by a dinner (necessarily in the old Hall), in which, in the course of an exceptionally witty speech, Derek Roe pointed out that Godfrey left the College 'with our student numbers well up to the permitted maximum of 75 and capital of our own of some 2.6 million, even after having spent 600,000 pounds in connection with the move. Were your immediate successors to continue progress at that rate, we should in quite a short while become the richest college in Oxford and one of the largest.'

Two stages in the making of Godfrey Stafford's portrait by Aubrey Davidson Houston (1906–1995), commissioned on his retirement.

The third Master: Dick Repp

Godfrey's successor and third Master of the College, Richard (Dick) Repp, began his tenure on 1 October 1987. The *College Record* commented subsequently that 'The *Oxford Times* was eager to point out that we are the third college in Oxford currently to have an American-born head; it did not add that we are the only College never to have had an English one.' The new Master, a native of Pennsylvania whose *alma mater* was Williams College, came to St Cross from Linacre College, where he had been Senior Tutor, and was very experienced in the ways of the University (as was his wife Cathy). In a similar fashion to Godfrey Stafford in his early years at the College, Dick Repp was to combine the Mastership with his existing post, University Lecturer in Turkish History. As time proceeded, however, he shouldered many additional burdens within the University, including that of Pro-Vice-Chancellor, which gave him a much-respected voice throughout Oxford – a great advantage for a new and comparatively small College amid many collegiate big beasts. Already Dick's first speech at a Founders'

Feast, on 27 November 1987, demonstrated the strategic thinking that characterised his leadership: he drew attention to the significance of a recent report on graduate studies in the University, which made it clear that 'there must be a psychological shift in the University, and in some respects a shift in resources, to enable graduate studies … to take their proper place in the life of the University.'

The end of the 1980s was a clear time of transition in St Cross, partly and sadly through the deaths of some of those who were the College's greatest friends. On 27 October 1989, the first Master, Kits van Heyningen, died and on 17 July 1990 there followed the death of Audrey Blackman, who left the College not merely her residual estate but her spectacular collection of water-colours and her house and garden in Boars Hill. She would have liked to see 'Wood Croft' as a residence for the Master, but beautiful as the setting was, it lacked practicality, particularly in Oxford traffic. It was maintained by the College for the next twenty years as a student residence, with an annual Open Day when the garden's rhododendrons were at their best.

The first Master, Kits van Heyningen, in front of the entrance to St Cross College on St Giles, 1982

Audrey Blackman (1907–1990)

Audrey Blackman

Derek Roe wrote an obituary for Audrey in the *College Record* for 1991, of which the following is a summary: Audrey Babette Blackman was the daughter of Dr Richard Seligman and his wife Hilda (née McDowell). Her father's Jewish background and her mother's Irish Catholic one seemed an unlikely combination in the early years of the century, but her childhood in Surrey was exceptionally happy. There were strong artistic talents on both sides of the family, and her maternal grandfather, himself a sculptor, had arranged the British sculpture for the Paris Exhibition of 1851. Audrey herself painted from childhood and first experimented with clay modelling in her teens.

Music remained an inspiration throughout her life, but in the 1920s she returned to sculpting and studied for several years at Goldsmiths' College in London and at Reading University. She also plunged into the social whirl of 1920s London and met her husband, Geoffrey Emmet Blackman, recently down from Cambridge and then at Jealotts Hill Research Station of ICI, just beginning his distinguished career in the agricultural sciences.

LEFT: *Op. 2, Encaenia 1* (1979) by Audrey Blackman (1907–1990), representing Audrey and Geoffrey Blackman at, or returning home from, an Encaenia Garden Party.

RIGHT: The garden at Wood Croft in Boars Hill, Oxford

LEFT: *Turkish Fortress at Delvino, Albania* (1856–7), by Edward Lear (1812–1888).

OPPOSITE: *All Saints Church, Walsoken, Norfolk* (1817), by John Sell Cotman (1782–1842).

BELOW: *Bombed, St John's, Waterloo Road* (ca 1941), by John Piper (1903–1992), showing the interior of the parish church of St John's Waterloo Road. All from the Blackman Collection of Watercolours at St Cross College.

The large wild garden at their home on Putney Hill brought a love of gardening into Audrey's life which she never lost, even if it began as loyal support for a passion of her husband's. She did war work in London through the English-Speaking Union. Very soon after the war ended, her husband was appointed to the Sibthorpian Chair in Rural Economy at Oxford, with a fellowship at St John's College. Audrey lived on Boars Hill for the rest of her life, as academic wife and practising artist, in circumstances which she regarded as idyllic. She had already begun to find bronze a frustrating medium for her work when a chance visit to the Ashmolean Museum turned her attention to ceramic figures. She went to study ceramic techniques at the Oxford School of Art with Gladys Grimshaw, subsequently evolving her own methods of making rolled figures in porcelain with marbled, inlaid and impressed decoration, using stained clays in many colours. For the last ten years of her life, Audrey was a member of Common Room at St Cross: she greatly enjoyed the informal and friendly atmosphere there, making many friends among senior and junior members.

The South Wing at last

Audrey died just at the time when the College was celebrating its quarter-centenary. That anniversary began as a College Open Day on 3 June 1990, including a service in St Cross Church, and that was followed at the end of the month by dinner in a marquee in the Blackwell Quad, attended by Lord Jenkins of Hillhead as Chancellor. He was coming to a College which now had 115 students on its books, enough for the College to think rather tentatively of instituting regular evening meals on nights when there was no other event in Hall. On the eve of the half-century, however, the time had yet to come when the number of residents on site could provide the necessary critical mass.

At last, in 1991 there was a start on building for the South Wing, after the plans had finally been accepted by the planning authority. The principal architect was Philip del Nevo of Oxford Architects Partnership. Digging of foundations was preceded by an archaeological survey which did not reveal much of great significance, a disappointment for historians but a relief to those desperate to forward work already belated

1990: Jubilee celebration. *Left to right*: Ruth van Heyningen (founding fellow), Dick Repp (Master), Lord Jenkins (University Chancellor) and Alan Coates (DPhil student, later College archivist).

by more than half a decade. The first lunch in the new Hall was held on 11 January 1993. It was kitted out with tables and chairs to match those brought from the original Hall. On the floors above were twenty student bedrooms ready for occupation the next day, and there was an exercise room or mini-gym in the basement (it was converted into a TV room for students in the 2000s: *O tempora, o mores*). Marc Fitch had given a splendid Blüthner grand piano, historically associated with great names of the London musical scene in World War II (not least Dame Myra Hess), which still graces the completed Hall. It has to be said that the Blüthner is the chief beneficiary of the over-resonant acoustic, which is ideal for chamber concerts but excruciating for those of senior years when there are any substantial numbers at meals. Acoustical difficulties seem to be a recurrent curse of St Cross dining-halls.

Alterations to the old building, to create a new Common Room and surrounding conversions, could also now go ahead. The old Hall was renamed the Saugman Common Room, while the College Association provided funds to furnish the old Common Room as a study room, available at all hours (it was to be 'the Lange Quiet Room'!). Victorian writing tables and specially made mahogany chairs were provided – to be frank, characterised more by elegance than convenience for study. A sign of the times was that there was a computer terminal devoted to OLIS, which by now was beginning to include more and more of the College's own library. A beautiful oak bench in the garden, carved by Robert Thompson's legendary 'Mouseman' firm of carpenters, commemorated the tragic accidental

1991: the raw unfinished toothings of the old building and the mulberry tree, before building of the new wing commences.

BELOW: 1992: the new South Wing takes shape.

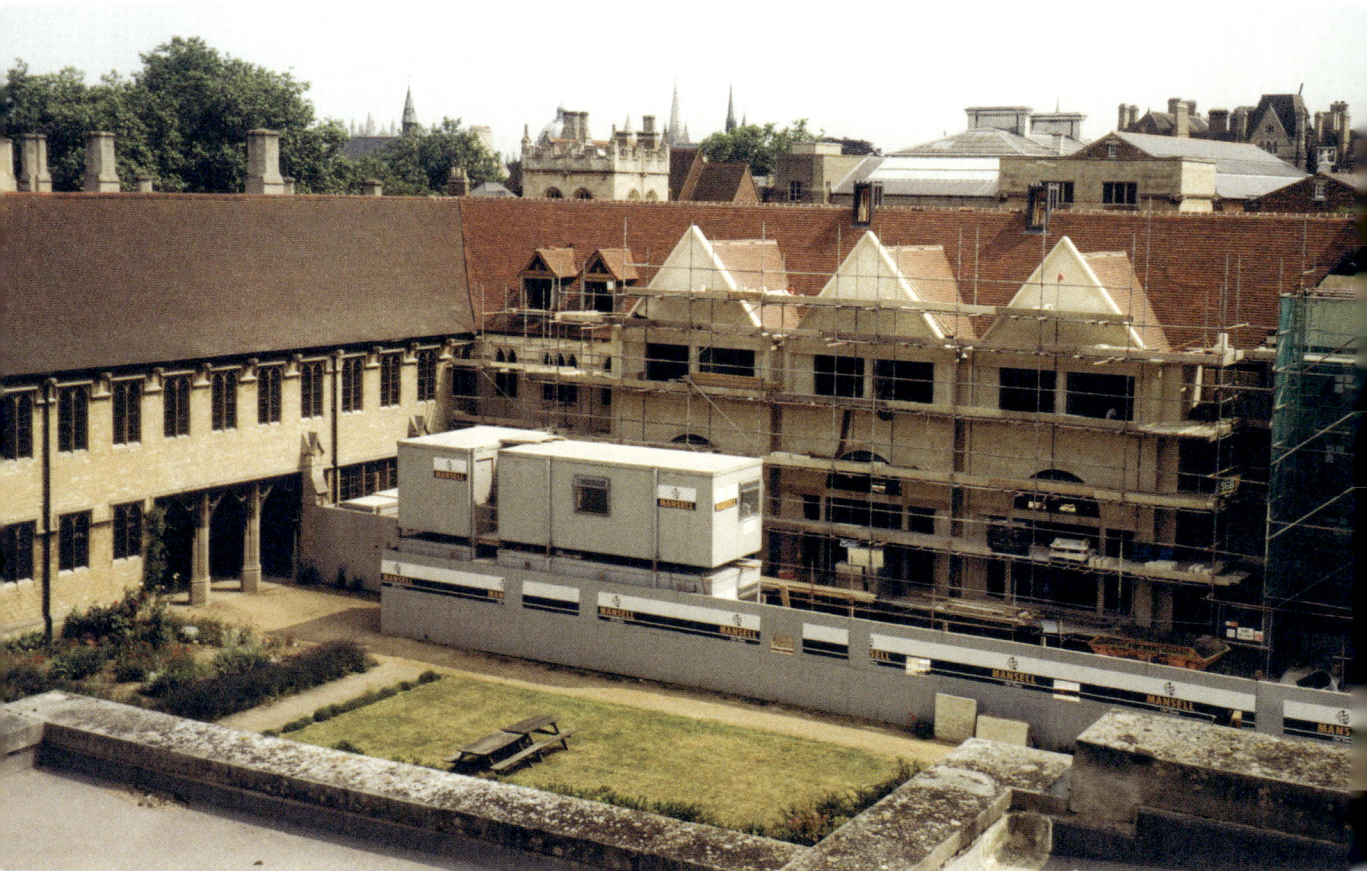

early death in 1992 of a Junior Research Fellow, Mark Hetherington; it was given by his parents, who also presented the College with a silver candelabrum in his memory.

Douglas Wigdor, two-year student for an M.Litt. in politics from 1993, reminisces fondly about this new period of maturity in the College's life: 'St Cross lunch was undoubtedly the best in Oxford and the collegiality was well known ... Everything you needed to know (and more) for most of the 90s could be ascertained by the College's friendly and gregarious porter Bob Vincent.' For his porter's lodge, poor Bob, though uncomplaining, was marooned with overflowing pigeon-holes in a virtually windowless upstairs room now considered just big enough for the College photocopier: not all the infrastructure of a 'proper' College was as yet quite in place.

The South Wing Gargoyles

Dr Frits W. Hondius (1927–2006) had a long and varied career in law and development. He was prominent in the administration of the Council of Europe and played a leading role in the development of European law on sustaining non-governmental (civil society) organisation. After a happy time as a visiting fellow of St Cross, he was inspired to commission two carved stone gargoyles, sculpted in France by François Saur, for the new South Wing of the College. Frits is seen here following the installation of the finished gargoyles, said (plausibly) to be the only specimens of Meso-American inspiration in Oxford. The drawings giving two views of each gargoyle are by Emilie Savage-Smith, 2009.

On 24 April 1993, Lord Jenkins was back to preside over an opening ceremony for all the new work, with an audience of around 200. A finely-illustrated booklet, in effect the first College history, was produced by the College's bursar Kenneth Hylson-Smith, along with David Sturdy and Brian Atkins, to mark this occasion. Dick Repp wrote at the end of the year that 'The simple recounting of the new facilities and of the use of them … does not perhaps do full justice to their importance. … they have, finally, added a proper physical dimension to the sense of collegiality which has always existed at St Cross … we believe we have now achieved that essential quantum of space and level of facilities which in the physical sense recognizably constitutes a College.'

Memorial Bench for Mark Hetherington.

Old site, new buildings

Well, it was more of a plateau than a quantum! Oxford horizons have a habit of very quickly expanding to fit institutional ambitions or emerging new needs. The Centre for Islamic Studies's move from the hut on St Cross Road opened up the old site for expansion, and a very adroit set of negotiations between a College with available land but little capital and a College in precisely the reverse situation resulted in 1995 in an unusual deal. Brasenose College and St Cross would jointly develop the old College site on St Cross Road, as both Colleges were desperate for more graduate student accommodation. Naturally, although the handsome Kirby Old School was kept as part of the scheme, incorporating a flat for a site supervisor, the faithful hut must finally go, and in July 1995, the College's first home was at last demolished to begin work for pile-driving.

Summer 1995: the hut is demolished, ending an era.

BELOW: The new St Cross Road buildings take shape

Some fellows of St Cross thought that during the demolition, their cherished mulberry tree, once a source of academic grazing and of Mrs Helliwell's magnificent mulberry tarts, had been lost. It had stood just outside the wooden hut, and was the only residue of the old St Cross vicarage garden. Yet after all the upheaval, there it still is, flourishing between the two residential buildings of Brasenose and St Cross. By contrast, another mulberry that was in the back garden of Pusey House was definitely sacrificed when the new dining hall was built in the early 1990s. The plan now is to take cuttings from the tree on the 'old site' and plant them on the St Giles site as a restitution for past loss.

"

Some fellows of St Cross thought that during the demolition, their cherished mulberry tree, once a source of academic grazing and of Mrs Helliwell's magnificent mulberry tarts, had been lost.

"

On a mercifully fine day on 25 September 1996, the Colleges held a joint ceremony to open the new building on the old site. The St Cross building, appropriately enough approximately cruciform, stands on the southwestern part of the site, while the Brasenose building makes up the rear at the eastern and part of the northern boundaries, in a rough quadrangle, with the Old School House at the entrance. The new St Cross block gave 49 student rooms to the College, providing major relief to the situation in which the College could only house twenty-nine per cent of its students (though since then, expanding numbers have once more made new demands).

The formal part of the celebration took place in the parish church of St Cross, the last time that the College would use it – it is now mostly converted into an Historic Collections centre for Balliol College. Despite the ecclesiastical setting, a meeting of St Cross Governing Body had rather emphatically decided against involving any notable ecclesiastical dignitary, so the opening was performed by the Master of St Cross and the Principal of Brasenose simply jointly declaring the building open, in a ragged but rousing unison, whereupon the party spilled out on to the new space between its two buildings for a commemorative drink or two with a buffet lunch. In the evening there followed a celebration dinner in St Cross for the Governing Bodies of both Colleges: it must be said that St Cross was better represented at this than Brasenose, for whom it was naturally not such a climactic

occasion in their rather longer history. Another booklet by indefatigable historian Kenneth Hylson-Smith commemorated the opening. As a result of this expansion of accommodation, by 1997 the numbers of students on the College's books reached about 180, ten times what they were when St Cross had moved to its St Giles site.

Here, then, was a major moment of achievement in the College's growth, a fitting culmination to two decades of very rapid change. One equally momentous change during 1996–7 was necessarily less trumpeted, and indeed negotiated by Dick Repp with his usual tact and strategic vision. It marked the end of one of the possible strategies for the future which, as we have seen, had initially been prominent in this Phase Two of the College's life. By the late 1990s the Centre for Islamic Studies and the Centre for Hebrew and Jewish Studies were both well-established in their own right, while for the time being, there was no Christian-based counterpart to them, since the Ian Ramsey Centre had drawn in its horns (before its new independent lease of life in recent years). Accordingly, the College Governing Body took the decision to bring to an end, 'in an entirely amicable manner', as Dick Repp reported in the *College Record*, '… the quasi-formal status of our Associated Centres … both have now grown into well-established, independent institutions with their own well-defined purposes and aims, and an honest reappraisal of the relationships by all concerned concluded that the links now had too little substance to justify formal association.' Some (not all) members of the Centres remained fellows of the College, and it remains the case, and should be a source of pride in the College, that it was a founding fellow who was the founding director of the Oxford Centre for Hebrew and Jewish Studies; and that the founding director of the Oxford Centre for Islamic Studies remains an emeritus fellow of the College. Nevertheless, what that decision meant is that unlike some other graduate Colleges, St Cross had made a conscious decision not to specialise in terms of discipline or academic orientation. In its academic interests, as well as the intake of its student body and its fellowship alike, it has subsequently opened itself, in the felicitous Latin recommended for its motto by Peter Glare and John Tiffany, *Ad quattuor cardines mundi* – 'To the Four Corners of the Earth.'

OVERLEAF: The new South Wing in the west quad of the St Giles site, 2013.

A FEELING OF PERMANENCE
1996–2014

Jan-Georg Deutsch

By 1996, the new student accommodation on St Cross Road was open and the College occupied, at least in part, two sites in the City of Oxford. The following essay provides a brief narrative outline of the major developments that have occurred in the eighteen years since that time. This is augmented by a number of vignettes that emphasize the emergence of the College as a fully-fledged University institution, something that the founding fellows had hoped for, but which few believed could be actually achieved within their lifetime. Like all histories of the present, for better or worse, recounted lived experience is more often than not an exercise in interpretation rather than a dispassionate account of a more distant past, since so much depends on one's personal recollections. This brief account of St Cross College between 1996 and 2014 will be no exception.

At first sight, the late 1990s and 2000s seem to be particularly uneventful. No further 'Wings' or 'Annexes' were opened, or huts or mulberry trees destroyed, though there were some notable building activities in this period, such as the construction in 2005 of the College Lodge, including the Mail Room, enabling the College for the first time to employ an evening porter. There was also the creation of the St Cross Room and the relocation of the Van Heyningen Room, the latter being moved from the first floor in the St Giles building to the ground floor. That room now holds part of the library collection and serves as a venue for special dinners and doctoral examinations. The new St Cross Room is where Governing Body now meets. It also houses cases displaying

The chapel of Pusey House seen through a door of the Saugman Common Room, 2013.

some of the Treverton Trust ceramics, figurines by Audrey Blackman and the antique glass collection on permanent loan from Derek Roe.

However, the perspective that these two decades were uneventful is deceptive. After all, during this time two new Masters were elected: Andrew Goudie in 2003 and Mark Jones in 2011.

Moreover, the period also saw a number of crucial incremental changes, which, while not tied to specific events, had a considerable impact. Among them, one should count, first, the significant improvement in personal communication between St Cross College and Pusey House. While, as the then Master Andrew Goudie wrote in the *College Record*, 'for more than a quarter of a century relations have not always been harmonious', arguably referring to the sharply contrasting views that had emerged over practical decision-making, the 'breaking out of peace and goodwill between Pusey and St Cross' from the mid-2000s seemed to have eased greatly any tension that might have existed between the two in the past. As a result, the College was able to acquire from Pusey House a significant portion of the freehold of the site, which was seen as indispensable for the unencumbered future development of the College, particularly its physical facilities.

ABOVE LEFT: The College Lodge, 2014, with Paul Wicking, Head Porter.

ABOVE RIGHT: The St Cross Room, refurbished in 2006 as a meeting room for the Governing Body.

OPPOSITE: The Van Heyningen Room, 2013 .

Portrait Making: The Third Master, Richard (Dick) Repp

Commissioned by the College, the portrait was painted in oils by Juliet Wood, an acclaimed British artist. She had studied at the St Albans School of Art under Norman Adams and at the Slade School of Fine Art under Sir William Coldstream (who had earlier painted Kits van Heyningen's portrait). She has exhibited in many places, including the Royal Society of Portrait Painters, the Royal Academy and Scottish National Portrait Gallery. The portrait was first shown in 2000, three years before Dick Repp retired. The cost of the painting was met by members of the College, in response to an appeal by the Vice-Master of the time. Dick Repp, who seemed mildly diverted by the whole proceedings, including the twelve sittings for the painting, was certainly happy with the final result.

OPPOSITE: The portrait of Richard (Dick) Repp (Master, St Cross College, 1987–2003) by Juliet Wood, 2000.

BELOW: Juliet Wood working on Dick Repp's portrait.

Portrait Making: The Fourth Master, Andrew Goudie

The creation of Andrew Goudie's portrait was an entirely different undertaking. Originally the College had in mind to commission a portrait from a professional painter. To everyone's surprise and joy, however, the then Senior Tutor, Kate Scott, who happened to have studied for a Fine Art degree in her youth, volunteered to have a go at it, and what a marvellous result came out of that! The portrait was done in oils, the vibrant background colours referring to one of Andrew Goudie's favourite places on earth (as a geographer by profession he has seen many of them!), the Namib Desert in coastal Southern Africa. Initially, she had in mind painting him leaning against a Land Rover in the desert, but better sense prevailed. Kate Scott described her experience of producing the painting as truly enjoyable and so did Andrew Goudie. The College is privileged in having a painting that so well displays the lively personality of the sitter.

The portrait of Andrew Goudie (Master, St Cross College 2003–2011) by Kate Scott, 2010.

A significant symptom of the 'normalisation' of the atmosphere in the two institutions was that the new Principal of Pusey, Fr Jonathan Baker, invited the College to hold its annual Carol Service in Pusey Chapel once more, after some years during which the occasion had been exiled to St Giles parish church. Back in this setting, it has become one of the highlights of College life.

Equally important is the fact that in the late 1990s and early 2000s a vision came to fruition that had been formed much earlier – namely, that the College might acquire a sense of perpetuity and respectability that most took as the hallmark of a University of Oxford College. From its very beginning the fellows of St Cross had wished the College to become a fully recognised institution of the University. This was, however, an uphill struggle. The founding of St Cross in 1965 was perceived by some at that time to be a challenge to the established authorities running the University. An example is the then Warden of Wadham College, Maurice Bowra, who, perhaps in reference to the South African background of Kits van Heyningen, could apparently not

17 October 2007: A celebration of a new agreement between St Cross College and Pusey House. *Left to right*: Fr Jonathan Baker, Principal of Pusey House, who subsequently became the Bishop of Fulham; Rev. William Davage, David Browning, and Andrew Goudie (Master).

resist calling the non-fellows' movement for the establishment of one or more new Colleges 'the revolt of the Kaffirs.' Times have luckily changed in many respects, as such language and perspective would be deemed to be unacceptable now – even for the Head of House of an Oxford College – but it is important to keep in mind that fifty years ago such reactionary sentiments were not uncommon and were an important part of the backdrop to the formation, vision and development of St Cross College over the years.

When the St Cross Road Annexe was opened in 1996 the then Master Dick Repp proudly proclaimed that 'The College has finally achieved what is in other contexts often called a "minimum kit" with respect to physical plant.' However, it was arguably only in the later 1990s and early 2000s that the vision of the founders finally became reality: when the 'physical plant' acquired a distinctive social life, that is when the majority of the 'traditions' were invented and developed that today make St Cross a special place rather than merely a physical space. Invented traditions are, as the British historian Eric Hobsbawn put it, 'practices […] of a ritual or symbolic nature that seek to inculcate certain values and norms of behaviour' in order to create what one might call a 'moral community.' What this meant in the context of the making of St Cross and how this was achieved is the main part of the story which, in the form of some vignettes, this essay seeks to tease out from the College records and personal recollections.

The following account highlights the remarkable internal, largely incremental, transformation that the College experienced in the period under review. In the late 1980s the College was still seen by many of its members primarily as a fellows' College, perhaps not without good reason as the foundation of the College had its origin in the aforementioned non-fellows' movement, also known informally as the non-don movement, and when the College opened it consisted only of fellows, being joined the following year by only six students. After the College's foundation there were a number of years when a sizeable number of active College fellows had still vivid personal memories of their involvement in the foundation of St Cross and regarded it – more or less – as their personal achievement. Twenty years later their numbers had significantly declined. Largely due to retirement, by the

The last four Masters of the College: *Left to right*: Richard 'Dick' Repp (third Master, 1987–2003), the current Master Sir Mark Jones, the fourth Master Andrew Goudie (2003–2011), and Godfrey Stafford (second Master, 1979–1987).

early 2000s there was not a single Governing Body Fellow left who had personal recollections of the foundations of the College. Surely this must have had an impact on the atmosphere in the College, although few in this period, as far one can tell from the *College Record,* might have noticed it.

Moreover, in the 1980s the College employed only a few full-time administrators. The first bursar, Kenneth Knowles, for instance, was still a teaching fellow in economics and statistics who out of a sense of duty had agreed to take up the post of bursar. As the number of students increased in the 1990s and 2000s, however, this part-time approach to administration was no longer viable. The administrative staff had to be fully professionalised in order to keep the College functioning. In this connection one might mention that the College was fortunate in employing a number of highly competent professional administrators, as in the case of the current bursar, Maureen Doherty, who, following in the footsteps of her predecessors, managed the administrative transformation of the College in the later 1990s and early 2000s with great skill and little fuss.

Bursar Maureen Doherty, 2013.

The number of graduate students admitted to the College greatly increased, largely as a result of the expansion of graduate studies, particularly one-year courses, in the University as a whole. The expansion of student numbers at St Cross in particular was the result of a conscious policy, vigorously pursued, partly for financial reasons, by Dick Repp, Master from 1987 to 2003, and by Andrew Goudie, who succeeded him as Master of the College from 2003 to 2011. Both sought to develop St Cross into a fully-established graduate college of the University. This needed significant resources and, in the absence of a large donation, it could only be achieved through greater student numbers. In 1996 the College comprised about 70 fellows and 165 students. Ten years later, in 2006, these numbers had increased to about 80 fellows and 320 students. By 2014 the College had about 100 fellows and over 500 students, about half of whom were women. The gender balance of the community, in terms of both the fellows and the students, is one of the best among all Oxford colleges.

In 1996 the College comprised about 70 fellows and 165 students. Ten years later, in 2006, these numbers had increased to about 80 fellows and 320 students. By 2014 the College had about 100 fellows and over 500 students.

To cut a long story short, to an outsider it appeared that the College had changed its character. By the early 2010s the erstwhile rather sedate 'fellows' club' in St Cross Road had metamorphosed into a lively 'students' hub' in St Giles.

Yet there was also an external dimension to this transformation over which the College had little influence or control, but which strongly affected its substance and outlook. This was the changing context in which Oxford Colleges have operated during the last two decades, both within the University and within British academia at large. A major issue here was the implementation of extensive administrative reforms within the University in the late 1990s and early 2000s following a review of the organisation of the University chaired by the then Vice-Chancellor, Sir Peter North. Major changes to the internal structure of the University were introduced in October 2000. The University's two principal governing committees – the Hebdomadal Council and the General Board of the Faculties – were merged into

Splendour In The Rain:

Colleges in Oxford – as is well known – have their own time frames. Of course, there is the annual coming and going of students and fellows, but the decades are punctuated by different events, notably the election of a new Master (a process that is not entirely dissimilar from the hysterical drama surrounding the election of a new Pope) and the appointment of a fellow to high university office, especially to be a Proctor or Assessor. These posts are held on rotation among the Colleges and thus the honour of nominating a proctor or assessor happens only very infrequently, that is to say about every fifteen years. Apart from being a member of all University key decision-making committees, the Assessor is responsible for student welfare and finance across the University. In March 2005, it was the turn of St Cross, and Frank Pieke (an anthropologist by training, which prepared him well for the job!) was duly elected from St Cross. The inauguration was a splendid affair. It consisted of a procession of members of the College, including the Master, fellows and representatives of the students from the College, to Convocation House in full academic regalia. It started all well, but then the rain made 'doing' splendour a little bit more difficult. Perhaps making up for it, after the ceremony a truly spectacular formal lunch was held at the College, to which University as well as personal guests of the new Assessor were invited.

Procession in rain for installation of the Assessor, 2005.

a single Council, while the faculties, sub-faculties, and departments were regrouped into five new and increasingly potent academic divisions that were subsequently reduced to four. The demise of the Hebdomadal Council and General Board was mourned by few. They were seen by many observers as being no longer fit for the purpose of governing the expanding University, which had become ever more Byzantine both in structure and, indeed, politics. In the process of reforming the University, however, the Colleges lost some aspects of their pre-eminence in the University, while 'Wellington Square' (as the University central administration and its divisional ancillary services are widely known) gained greater significance in University affairs. Power in the University has gradually swung away from the academics in the Colleges and the Faculties towards administrators and managers in the administration, notably towards the Heads of Division and the Pro-Vice-Chancellors, who are not elected by Congregation (traditionally defined as 'The Masters and Scholars of the University') but, rather, are appointed by the Vice-Chancellor. For good or ill, as a result, the erstwhile 'collegiate', and some would argue dysfunctional, University structure had become much more centralised.

Moreover, and arguably even more decisively, with the expansion of graduate studies and the reforms determining the distribution of government funding among UK universities in the 1990s (the so-called 'research assessment exercises'), departmental as well as individual research activities – as opposed to College-based undergraduate teaching – became much more highly valued. Consequently, those fellows who are primarily engaged in research and graduate teaching or University administration had very few incentives, and perhaps also less time, to become closely involved in seemingly parochial, and in career terms less rewarding, College affairs.

As a result, when in the early 2000s St Cross finally managed to become a fully-established Oxford College (with its 'physical plant' and 'invented traditions' in place) the University itself was changing. The transformation of the University and external developments, however, affected Colleges in Oxford in different ways. As a graduate College of recent origin, St Cross was probably spared some of the adjustment pain of the more traditionally-oriented undergraduate Colleges. But in general, it is also clear that these changes undermined, at least in part, the rationale for the very existence of Colleges in a more centrally-administered and research-driven 'collegiate University.' The Colleges as a whole were no longer able to enjoy the kind of unique prestige and perhaps communal sense of purpose and loyalty they were accustomed to in the past. Whether one welcomes these changes or not, from this perspective it is not difficult to see that for St Cross – as for any other College in the University – the question of how to reconcile the contradictions between internal development and external pressures was and will be a serious and enduring matter of concern.

In the mid-2000s the College had begun to respond to these concerns by significantly increasing its fundraising efforts, especially among its alumni, with the aim of completing the West and North Wings. Improving communications with the growing number of former students thus assumed high priority. The decision to add to the College's buildings was partly due to the dearth of student accommodation, which had by that time become a pressing problem following the rise in the numbers of students admitted to the College. But the decision to undertake the completion of the west or 'second quad' was also guided by a suggestion of the then Master, Andrew Goudie, that St Cross should become a '24-hour College.' This, he argued, would enable the College to offer regular dinners in the evenings as well as social and academic events that would make it more attractive to students and fellows alike. At the time of writing it remains to be seen whether this strategy will be ultimately successful, both in terms of completing the 'second quad' and strengthening the distinctive St Cross culture so as to thrive in the 'brave new world' of British Higher Education. If the current Master, Sir Mark Jones, who took up the post in 2011 following a successful tenure as director of the V&A Museum, is blessed with the same kind of good fortune that his predecessors enjoyed, one can only be optimistic about the future of the College.

Vignettes

The transformation of St Cross from being primarily a functional space into a social place did not actually start in 1996, as both the previous contributions to this volume have clearly shown. From the very beginning, all the Masters had sought to infuse the College with a degree of enjoyment and social life. An example is the establishment by the first Master of the College, Kits van Heyningen, of 25 October, or St Crispin's Day, as the day to mark the foundation of the College through prayers of thanksgiving. This event is today merged with the 'Founders' Feast', held at the end of each Michaelmas Term to commemorate the creation of the College. Yet from the early 1990s the speed, range and depth of the implementation of socially useful 'invented traditions' notably increased. A significant number of the College 'traditions' celebrated today were indeed invented (or revived, as the case may be) only in the 1990s and early 2000s. Some of these innovations and inventions are explored below.

The Common Room just after lunch, 2013.

To the Four Corners of the World

The armillary sundial in the College garden was made by David Harber and inaugurated in June 1999. It was a gift by the family of a former student of the College, Ronald Hurst, who had died before the completion of his doctoral thesis (more about him below). Its acquisition prompted a reappraisal of the layout of the second quad. The then Garden Master, Suke Wolton, together with Walter Sawyer, Superintendent of the University Parks, produced a wonderful scheme for the improvement of the garden in order to provide a proper setting for the armillary sphere sundial. Sadly, due to lack of funds, the full plans could not be realised, but the sundial has found its recognised place in the garden. The seating arrangements around the armillary sundial proved to be hugely popular with the students and indeed fellows, who often take their lunches there. Weather permitting, some fellows even conduct their tutorial teaching in the 'square'.

The armillary sundial provided the basis for the eventual crest of the College and its motto: To the Four Corners of the World, *ad quattuor cardines mundi*. For the College, the motto symbolised the increasing internationalisation of its cosmopolitan student body, habitually toing and froing between St Cross and every other conceivable place in the world. In fact, the number of countries represented among St Cross students during the last couple of years has totalled more than a hundred and twenty.

OPPOSITE: Armillary sundial forged by David Harber and given to the College in 1999 in memory of former student Ronald Hurst.

For the family of Ronald Hurst, however, the sphere referred more to the fact that he was an aviator of great distinction, who had seen many parts of the world. He was truly a mature student, for he came to St Cross at the age of seventy-one. He began work on a thesis concerned with eighteenth-century American history, but changed to a topic that much better reflected his experience in the RAF during the Second World War and his subsequent career in the aviation industry. In his thesis he set out to explore the career of a certain Charles Grey, a rather controversial figure who was the founding editor of the foremost aviation journal at the time, *The Aeroplane*. Sadly, due to illness he was unable to finish his work, but those who had the privilege of meeting him attested to his 'perpetual youthfulness, an uncontrollable sense of fun, [and] a delight in discovery', which, to my mind at least, could serve admirably as an unofficial motto for the College as a whole.

The armillary sphere in the garden is inscribed with a poem by the British writer James Elroy Flecker (1884–1915) taken from his verse drama titled *Hassan: The Story of Hassan of Baghdad and How he Came to Make the Golden Journey to Samarkand*, for which Frederick Delius composed the incidental music. The inscription reads:

> *We travel not for trafficking alone,*
> > *By hotter winds our fiery hearts are fanned.*
> *For lust of knowing what should not be known,*
> > *We take the Golden Road to Samarkand.*

Again, not a bad motto for a College!

Theft and a Bit of Luck

Occasionally, having some misfortune turns out to be all for the good. The College possesses a small, but well-loved silver collection. Given that the College was established only fifty years ago, it has some fine decorative vessels and utensils of silver. The College has obtained these items largely by gift, either in connection with the founding of St Cross or later. The College was quite keen to extend its collection, since, as the then Master, Godfrey Stafford, put it: 'No Oxford College is complete without its silver.'

Preliminary line-drawings for the ornamental dishes by Rebecca de Quin, 2003.

A pair of non-matching silver fruit dishes, one round and one oval, by Rebecca de Quin, London, 2003.

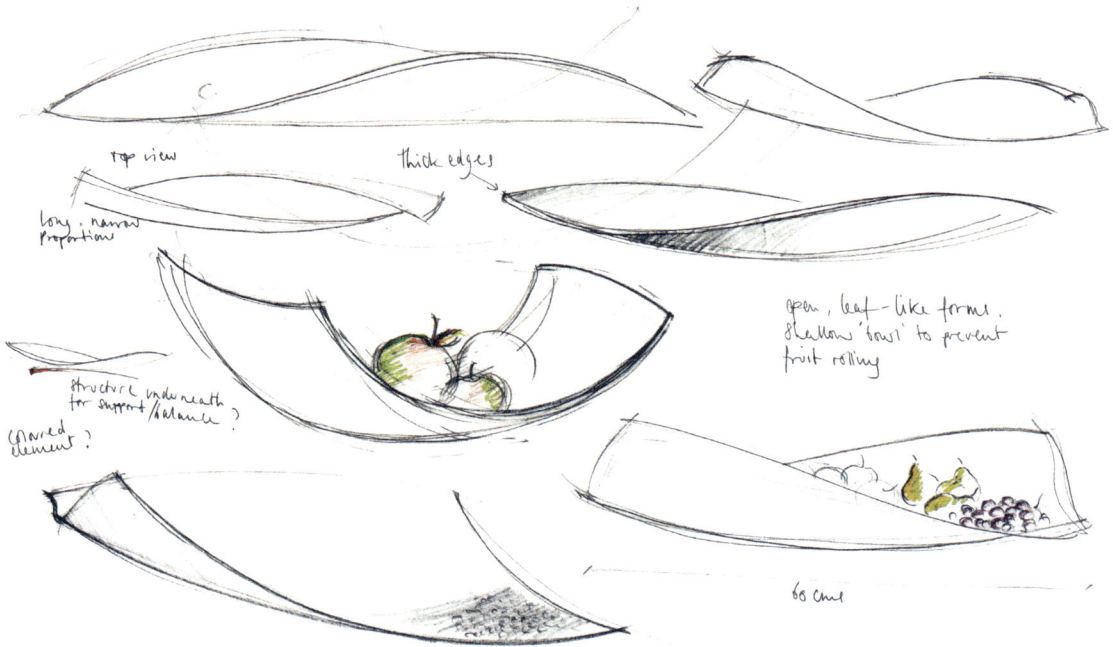

① shallow fruit dishes — a pair

top view
thick edges

long, narrow
proportion

open, leaf-like forms.
shallow 'bowl' to prevent
fruit rolling

structure underneath
for support/balance ?

coloured
element ?

60 cms

RdeQuin 01

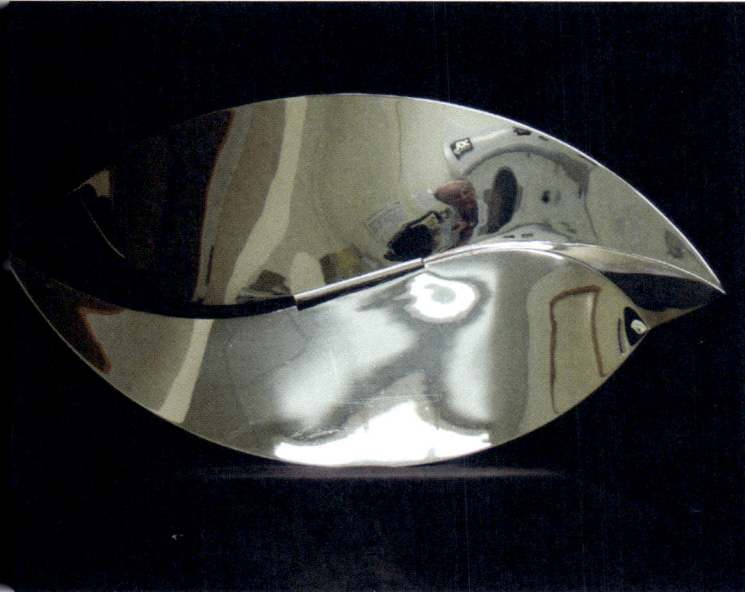

DECORATION TO HAVE INLAID FINES
GOLD DETAILS ~

GILT INTERIOR.

POLISHED EDGES

SILVER DISH WITH GILT INTERIOR ~ CHASED CROSS DECORATION OF SKIPPER
BUTTERFLIES AND MULBERRY LEAVES AND FRUITS ~

SQUARE SILVER DISH ~ PLAN VIEW ~
MULBERRY AND FRUITS WITH SKIPPER BUTTERFLIES ~

CHASED DECORATION ~

GILT INTERIOR ~

ST CROSS COLLEGE

RICH KELLY/G 2001

SILVER FOOT

In July of 1999, however, thieves entered the College at night, more specifically the Lange Room (the Library), where some of the College silver was on display. Somewhat bafflingly, the burglars only stole a very few pieces, but among them was a fine and important Arts and Crafts table centrepiece of silver and enamel (a shallow bowl, raised on a short foot and stem) designed by C. R. Ashbee sometime around the First World War. It had been acquired by the College through the Mildred Treverton Trust. Fortunately, the pieces were heavily insured, which allowed Governing Body to indulge in replacing them with new purchases. Although the College was a little short of money at the time, it took the praiseworthy decision not to put the insurance money into the general reserve. Moreover, rather than buying antique silver with the insurance funds, Governing Body took the bold step of commissioning as replacements one or two pieces of contemporary silver art work, for display at dinner and other formal occasions. Naturally, Governing Body left the whole business of sorting out the practicalities to the

College Arts Committee and its capable chairman Derek Roe, who had a particular interest in silver. Commissioning art work is actually not an easy task, not least because it is very difficult for even two people to agree, let alone an entire Arts Committee or, for that matter, an Oxford College Governing Body, about what truly constitutes beauty, especially 'modern' beauty. Anyway, the results were (and are!) remarkable, even if they took another four years, until 2003, to materialise. But it was worth the wait. The artists, Rod Kelly and Rebecca de Quin produced some outstanding works, which are elegant and highly pleasing to the eye.

Respectability at last: The College Coat of Arms

One of the most important steps towards the development of a corporate identity for St Cross was the successful application to the College of Arms for a Grant of Arms. Earlier attempts in 1983 to obtain a Grant were, as has been noted above, not at all encouraging. However, with the granting of Arms to other Colleges, notably Green College and Kellogg College in the early 1990s, St Cross became the only College in the University which did not have a Coat of Arms. Perhaps that would not have mattered that much to the University, were it not for the fact that not having a Coat of Arms stood out as a grave deficiency, notably in the *University Calendar*, which carried a half-blank page in the 1990s under the heading of St Cross where normally the arms were shown. Moreover, St Cross students thought it was odd that of all Oxford Colleges only St Cross was deprived of any easily recognisable symbols. In 1996, the College approached the University again, and this time the latter relented.

The ultimate success in obtaining the College Coat of Arms owes much to the tenacity and resourcefulness of John Tiffany, College fellow and former Lecturer in Ophthalmological Biochemistry. It was not an easy task, lobbying the University on behalf of St Cross from as early as 1980 (having formed with another senior member of St Cross, Paul Morgan, the College Sub-Committee for Heraldic Affairs) and then steering the debate about what the future Coat of Arms should look like towards a durable consensus in Governing Body.

A Coat of Arms has four distinct elements: a shield, a motto, a crest, and a badge. Finding a design for the shield – purple cross

John Tiffany, responsible for the design of the Crest, Badge, and successful awarding of the Grant of Arms.

potent on a silver ground, with the first quarter counter-changed – was comparatively stress-free. The design was basically the same that had been used previously as a logo on a windscreen parking sticker when St Cross was still housed in the old buildings in St Cross Road. The then

The Letters Patent, the official Grant of Arms for St Cross College, dated 'the year of Our Lord Two Thousand' and signed P. Ll. Gwynne-Jones, *Garter*, D.H.B. Chesshyre *Clarenceux*, and Thomas Woodcock, *Norroy and Ulster*.

bursar Kenneth Knowles seems to have suggested this design as he is believed to have found a similar pattern somewhere in St Cross Church, or possibly the Old School House on the site. The sticker design proved popular and, even before the official Coat of Arms was granted, it had appeared in various guises on a number of College paraphernalia. The motto *ad quattuor cardines mundi* was suggested by Peter Glare, resident Latinist and College fellow at the time, and was readily accepted by Governing Body as it emphasised the international character of the student body.

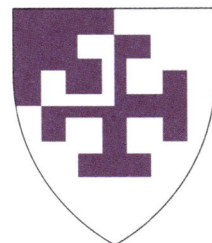

The Shield of St Cross College.

More difficult, indeed controversial, was the design of the crest. After much discussion in Governing Body the College settled for a golden armillary sphere modelled on the one in the garden. It was to be surmounted by a white dove standing on top of the sphere, carrying a sprig of a mulberry tree in its beak. In John Tiffany's words, the dove 'could be taken to indicate our desire to spread peace throughout the world, but one might equally see it, rather like Noah's dove and olive branch, as referring to our flight from St Cross Road to St Giles.' The significance of the mulberry sprig is also somewhat ambiguous: it could refer either to the mulberry tree that was a prominent feature of the College grounds on St Cross Road (which can still be seen today between the two buildings forming the St Cross/Brasenose Annexes) or to the mulberry tree that once flourished in the garden in the west quadrangle of the St Giles site. The latter was felled in order to make room for the new Hall, though the Oxford University Parks Department is said to still retain a cutting of that tree for us. Either way, the design proved to be popular, particularly the shield, while the simpler design of the badge, being merely a 'cross potent in gold design, with the centre of each arm cut out' is less widely used. The Letters Patent, the official parchment containing both the written grant and a detailed and coloured drawing of the arms, were finally received in 2001, more than twenty years after the idea for a College Coats of Arms had first been mooted. A skilfully embroidered version of the Coat of Arms by Dr Nonny Tiffany is prominently displayed in the Hall. What now remains to be done (in symbolic though not heraldic terms) is to find a proper flagpole mounted high for the purpose of flying the College colours and shield. Hopefully, this and, one might add, obtaining financial independence from the University, will not take another twenty years!

The Crest of St Cross College.

The Badge of St Cross College.

Inventing Traditions: Feasts and Blades

On the occasion of the 'annual service' of thanksgiving for the past and prayers for the future, held to mark the foundation of the College – the 'St Crispin's Day Service' – in late October 1980, the then College Chaplain, John Barton remarked that 'in St Cross a practice of two years' standing is already a College tradition.' Ironically, the supposedly annual St Crispin's Day Service' turned out to be a relatively short-lived affair, since it was soon thereafter merged with the Founder's Feast held at the end of Michaelmas Term. However, John Barton was absolutely right in pointing out that an enduring tradition in College terms could sometimes have a very tenuous connection with the past. A latter-day observer is often unaware that a firm 'tradition' had in fact been invented or revived only quite recently. Who would have thought, for instance, that the first St Cross

CLOCKWISE: Summer ball 2007, Fred's lunch 2010, Encaenia Garden Party 2009 and Christmas lunch 2007.

College Choir at the Carol Service in 2007.

College Summer Ball was held only in 1996, that the beautiful gong which plays such a central role in the College dinners, announcing that 'dinner is served' has been there only since 2001, or that the first September Gaudy was held only in 2002?

Other traditions began in the 1980s – such as the 'Musical Soirée' (now called Musical Evening), the 'College Colloquium' and the ever popular Carol Service with the College Choir – and were continued in the early 2000s with sufficient enthusiasm to merit entries in the *College Record*. The early 2000s were also the time that saw the regularisation of the Christmas lunch, the establishment of the weekly 'Special Dinners' (which proved to be hugely popular with College members), as well as the inauguration of 'Fred's Lunch' – an Alumni lunch named after its instigator, Fred Hodcroft, one of the founding fellows of the College. So distinctive is the name of this alumni gathering that even now if you search for Fred's Lunch on the internet you are immediately taken to St Cross College. The Alumni Gaudy was established in 2003 and the Christmas Drinks Reception in London began in 2004. In 2008, Douglas H. Wigdor (one of the many former St Cross students who made highly successful careers in the USA, in his case, in law) was presented with the first 'Alumnus of the Year Award.' The first College photo competition was held as recently as 2010.

Not all traditions are of modern invention, however, for St Cross continues the medieval tradition of a College member reading a Latin Grace before and after formal dinners. The Grace used in College before dinner was specially composed by Peter Glare, sometime general editor of the *Oxford Latin Dictionary* and long-time fellow of St Cross. It and the concluding Grace (a standard medieval concluding Grace) appear alongside much more venerable College Graces, some of them indeed medieval, in R. H. Adams volume *The College Graces of Oxford and Cambridge*. It is only fitting that the silver Grace holder that is used at every formal dinner was made in 1990 for the Twenty-Fifth Anniversary of the College by John Tobin, College fellow and an accomplished amateur silversmith.

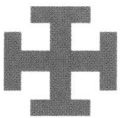

Latin Graces

The Latin Grace used in College before dinner was specially composed by Peter Glare:

Adesto nobis, Domine Deus noster: et concede ut quos Sanctae Crucis laetari facis honore, eius donis quoque salutaribus nutrias, per Dominum nostrum Iesum Christum. Amen.

(Be present to us, O Lord our God: and grant that those whom thou causest to delight in the honour of the Holy Cross, thou wilt also feed with its saving gifts, through Jesus Christ, Our Lord. Amen.)

At the request of Derek Roe, then Vice-Master, Peter Glare wrote at least one other Grace, for the retirement dinner for Godfrey Stafford as Master. In addition, Derek himself had written a Grace for the dinner on 12 November 1981 at which Harold Macmillan was the principal guest (the observant will notice its reference to the University motto):

Domine, illuminatio nostra et fons nostrae salubritatis, benedic nobis, oramus, necnon his donis, quae nunc ex tua liberalitate laetissimi sumpturi sumus, per Iesum Christum, Dominum nostrum. Amen.

(O Lord, our light and source of our health, bless us, we pray, together with these gifts which from thy bounty we are about to consume with the highest enjoyment, through Jesus Christ our Lord, Amen.)

'Crossfire' Blades,

Finally, one should mention that rowing, among other sports such as football, cricket and rugby, became a very popular student pastime from the early-2000s onwards. This might have been influenced by the fact that a former St Cross student, Tim Foster, actually won a gold medal in the Coxless Four competition at the Sydney 2000 Olympics, but it culminated in a spectacular showing at Summer Eights in 2007 and again in 2011, earning 'Blades' and the naming of a new boat ('Crossfire'), jointly owned by St Cross College and Wolfson College.

This list of College traditions is by no means comprehensive, but it shows that the 1990s and early 2000s were a particularly creative period for the invention of College traditions. It might be argued that this flourishing of College activities predominantly reflected the growth in student numbers or the sanguine, outgoing temperament of the personalities who were the Masters of the College at the time. Yet St Cross became a substantially different College in the late 1990s and early 2000s, not just with regard to its social life, but in all sorts of ways. In 1996, for instance, the College library received a generous five-year grant from Oxford University Press that enabled it to acquire enough current literature as well as reference books to develop into a proper, though relatively small, lending library.

OPPOSITE: College library on a busy afternoon, ca 2013.

Hélène La Rue and the College Gong

Hélène La Rue was a much loved College fellow, who sadly died after a short illness in July 2007. She was the curator of the Bate Collection of Musical Instruments of the University, and an extremely engaging and also very funny person – a great lover of cats, Morris Minors and Northumbrian bagpipes, and a key member of the College Choir. It was a privilege to know her. Among the many good things Hélène did for the College was to provide it with a proper gong. Until that gong arrived in 2002, the announcement that dinner was served was effected by a gentle tap on the Common Room door with a silver spoon. Civilised though it might have been, that method was neither particularly effective nor impressive. Thus the idea was raised by Cathy Repp, the wife of the then Master Dick Repp, that the College really needed something more useful for that purpose, such as a gong. As it happened, Hélène La Rue was sitting next to her at the dinner table. Hélène was at the time in the process of ordering new musical instruments to extend the Bate Collection, particularly its Gamelan section. Through her various connections, Hélène was able to establish contact with a famous gong maker near Solo in Java, Pak Tentrem, and Cathy and Dick Repp kindly agreed to donate a gong to the College.

Yet there was a problem: gongs in Java have great religious significance. Before someone can acquire one, the gong maker must be convinced that the instrument will not be used in a disrespectful manner. The gong maker was highly sceptical, but it was explained to him in some detail that the purpose of the gong would be only to call people to the dinner table. Having established that no harm was involved in that (considering our excellent wine cellar, one might dispute this!), he in fact became an enthusiastic supporter of the project, being extremely pleased by the prospect that an Oxford College would have a gong from his workshop. Making a gong is a lengthy skilful process which involves beating a large bronze disk slowly into shape and then fine-tuning it. It is only in the last stages of the production process that it becomes apparent to the maker that the gong will have a harmonious tone. Moreover, a suitable stand needed to be carved for it. It thus took some time for the gong and its stand to arrive from Java. It now proudly stands in the Common Room.

Hélène La Rue, 2005.

OPPOSITE: The Gong, made in Java by Pak Tentrem and donated in 2002 to the College by the then Master Dick Repp and his wife Cathy. Above the Gong is a portrait of Per Saugman, after whom the Common Room is named.

ST. CROSS COLLEGE

It can reasonably be said that by the early 2010s the vision of its founders that St Cross would develop into a significant institution within the University, fulfilling all the functions of an Oxford College with respect to its members, had been realized. In an institutional sense, only the formal legal standing that will come with independence remains to be achieved.

The College opened in 1965 as a graduate college with no students and forty-seven fellows, located in a small 'hut' and refurbished Victorian schoolhouse on St Cross Road. Fifty years on, it is situated in the centre of Oxford (on St Giles) in Edwardian buildings complemented by a handsome modern wing built in the 1990s and with some prospects of another wing soon to be built. The College now has about 100 fellows and over 500 students; however, they still share all facilities on equal terms, with no segregation at high table or in separate common rooms for senior or junior members. The remarkable changes that have transpired in these fifty years – not only with regard to the physical plant, but also in terms of its social life – arguably account for the strong sense of College community that exists today.

OVERLEAF: The entrance to the South Wing, opened in 1993, on the St Giles site, 2013.

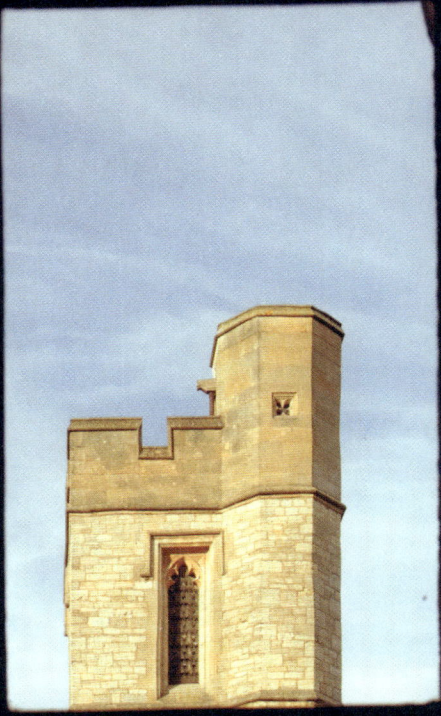

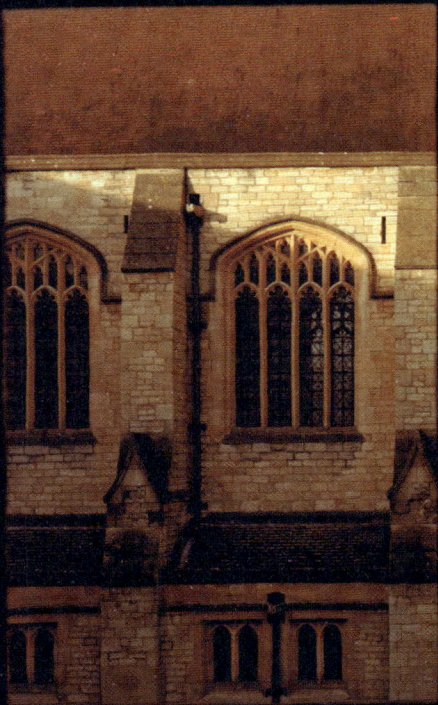

Acknowledgements

The authors and the editor have benefited greatly from many helpful suggestions, memorable recollections and old photographs offered by former and present members of College. In particular, they would like to thank the van Heyningen family for generously allowing various photographs to be used, including several taken by Ruth van Heyningen (one of the founding fellows) during the very early days of the College's existence. Substantial help was also forthcoming from Derek Roe (who has for many years tended the art collections of the College) and John Tiffany, who worked diligently on designing the coat of arms and related emblems used today to identify the College. Dick Repp and Andrew Goudie gave advice based on their extensive experience as former Masters of the College. Jim Williamson has for many years maintained and edited the *St Cross College Record*, which proved an invaluable source for the history of the College since 1980. Others have read all or parts of the present volume and rendered much-appreciated assistance: Sheila Allcock, Jo Ashbourn, John Barton, David Browning, Peter Benton, Dennis Britton, Michael Brookes, Alan Coates, Maureen Doherty, Margret Frenz, Alan Jones, Rana Mitter, Donald Richards, Bishop Geoffrey Rowell, and Brian Woolnough. The 'St Cross Archive Volunteer Group' – consisting of Lesley Forbes, Glenda Abramson and Hung Cheng – helped with checking particular details, while Glenda Abramson cast the eye of an experienced editor over the text as a whole. It goes without saying, however, that the many people who have offered assistance and encouragement should not be held responsible for any errors, misinterpretations or omissions.

Pusey House Chapel seen through the windows of the Accounts Office, 1st floor, St Giles site, 2013.

We would also like to thank the designer of the volume,
Isobel Gillan, for creatively weaving together our disparate materials.
Lesley Sanderson assisted the project in arranging for certain difficult
items in the archives and art collections to be photographed by Jeremy
Moeran. We also thank the Bodleian Library and the Oxfordshire
History Centre (Oxfordshire County Council) for supplying copies of
photographs and maps in their collections and for granting permissions
for their publication.

Tim Pound
Diarmaid MacCulloch
Jan-Georg Deutsch
Emilie Savage-Smith (editor)

Oxford, April 2014

Sources and Further Reading

Primary Sources

Freeborn, R.H., 'The Problem of Non-Fellows in Relation to the University and Colleges' (St Cross College Archives: X-2, Freeborn,1/4/61, typescript)

Browning, David: typescript history of the Oxford Centre for Islamic Studies

Manuscript volume compiled by W. E. van Heyningen recording *inter alia* accessions to the Mildred Treverton Trust Benefaction, with colour illus. Compiled ca 1980.

Miller, James, *Catalogue of British Drawings and Watercolours collected by Geoffrey and Audrey Blackman and bequeathed to St Cross College* (n.d. [1983], typescript)

Roe, Derek: typescript of memorial address for Godfrey Stafford, 18 October 2013

St Cross College Archives: D1/3/5; D1/1/3; D1/3/7; Z-4/1.29

Reminiscences deposited in College archives: Brian Atkins; Brent Jenkins; Jennifer Smith (now Baines); Eric Whittaker; Douglas Wigdor

Whittaker, Eric: typescript 'Recollections of a Hut Dweller' (St Cross College Archives: X-1, Whittaker, 4)

Published Sources

Adams, R. H. (ed.), *The College Graces of Oxford and Cambridge* (Oxford: Perpetua Press, 1992; Oxford, The Bodleian Library, 2013)

Clifford, Helen M., *A Treasured Inheritance: 600 Years of Oxford College Silver* [exhibition catalogue] (Oxford: Ashmolean Museum, 2004)

Crossword: The St Cross College Magazine (2005, p. 1; 2006, p. 1)

[Franks Report], *University of Oxford. Report of Commission of Inquiry. Vol. I: Report, Recommendations, and Statutory Appendix. Vol.II: Statistical Appendix* (Oxford: Clarendon Press, 1966)

Harrison, Brian (ed.), *The History of the University of Oxford. Vol. 8: The Twentieth Century* (Oxford: Clarendon Press, 1994) [esp. Robert Currie, 'The Arts and Social Studies, 1914–1939', p. 110; Jose Harris, 'The Arts and Social Sciences, 1939–1970', p. 218; Keith Thomas, 'College Life, 1945–1970', p. 211]

[Harrison Report] *Report on the closer integration of university teaching and research with the college system* (Supplement to the *University Gazette* no. 3214, 1962)

Hylson-Smith, Kenneth, *A History of Holywell and St Cross College/Brasenose College Residential Site* (Oxford: St Cross College, 1996)

Hylson-Smith, Kenneth, David Sturdy & Brian Atkins, *A History of St Giles and the St Cross College/Pusey House Site* (Oxford: St Cross College, 1993)

Irvine, Louise and Paul Atterbury, *Gilbert Bayes: sculptor 1872—1953* [exhibition catalogue] (Somserset: Richard Dennis, [1998]), pp. 98–9.

[Norrington Report, first] *Further report on the closer integration of university teaching and research with the college system* (Supplement no. 1 to the *University Gazette*, January 1964)

[Norrington Report, second] *Report of the committee appointed by the Hebdomadal Council to make detailed proposals for carrying out the policy contained in the further report on the closer integration of university teaching and research with the college system* (Supplement no. 1 to the *University Gazette*, November 1964)

Opie, Jennifer, *Ceramics in the Treverton Collection at St Cross College, Oxford* (Oxford: St Cross College, [2009])

Painting and Perception. MacRobert Centre Art Gallery, University of Stirling. Exhibition arranged by Andrew Forge. [exhibition catalogue] n.p., n.d. The William Coldstream, Nude, 1970, which at one time was in the collections of St Cross College, is illustrated on p. 334.

Roe, Derek, *A Note on the Antique Glass in the St Cross Room Cabinets* (Oxford: St Cross College [n.d.])

Roe, Derek, *The Art Collections of St. Cross College, Oxford, with particular reference to the Blackman Collection of English Watercolours*, by Derek Roe (Oxford: St Cross College, 2005)

Roe, Derek, *The Silver of St Cross College: a brief commentary*, 2nd edition, revised and illustrated (Oxford: St Cross College, 2010)

Roe, Derek, *The Blackman Collection of Watercolours at St Cross College, Oxford, with notes on the origins of the College's Art Collections, and on British Watercolours* (Oxford: St Cross College Arts Committee, 2013)

Sam Herman Glass. The Fine Art Society Ltd, London (Dec 1971 – Jan 1972) [exhibition catalogue] London, 1971.

St Cross College Record, issued nearly annually from 1980. In particular, 1980 (1), p. [28]; 1981 (2), p. [14, 18]; 1982 (3), pp. 32–36,40–41; 1984 (5), 29–30; 1985 (6), 1; 1988 (8), 25–27; 1990 (9), 40–42; 1991 (10), 13–15; 1993 (11), 24–26; 1994 (12), 17–20; 1996 (14), 14–16; 1997 (15), 40–42; 1998 (16), 18–19; 1999 (17), 17–19, 29–32; 2000 (18), 29–31; 2005 (22), 26–27; 2007 (24), 27; 2012 (29), 56.

The Telegraph, 8 May 2000

The Times, 5 April 1966

van Heyningen, W. E., *The Key to Lockjaw: an autobiography* (Gerrards Cross: Smythe, 1987)

van Heyningen, W. E., *The Founding of St Cross College: an interested account* (Oxford: Oxbow Books, 1988)

Index of Personal Names

Abraham, Sir Edward 90

Agas , Ralph 25

Allen, Philip 75

Andrews, Colin 74

Andrews, David G. 74, 75

Andrews, Margaret 75

Antill, Albert George 35

Ashbee, C. R. 131

Atkins, Brian 69, 102

Bagrit, Sir Leon 48

Baines, Jennifer (née Smith) 46, 47

Baker, Fr Jonathan 117, 118

Barbour, Ruth 35

Barton, John 59, 70, 72, 74, 80, 86, 87, 135

Bayes, Gilbert 52

Beckett, Philip 81, 84

Beckett, William Horton 35

Bennett, Canon Gareth (Garry) 71, 73

Berlin, Isaiah 22, 38

Betjeman, John 31, 49–51

Bialokoz, Jerzy Eugeniusz 35

Blackman, Audrey Babette 77, 82, 94–95, 112

Blackman. Geoffrey Emmet 77, 95

Blackwell, Sir Basil 42, 84–85

Blackwell, Miles 88

Blackwell, Richard 42, 60–61, 67, 85

Boyle, Robert 23

Bowra, Maurice 117

Britton, Dennis 35

Brookes, Michael 57, 59–60

Brown, George Malcolm 35

Browning, David 60, 87–88, 90, 118

Buckeridge, Charles 30

Burridge, Kenelm Oswald Lancelot 35–36

Clement, Tim 83

Clocksin, Bill 83

Coates, Alan 99

Coldstream, Sir William 54, 56-57, 114

Coles, Barry Arclay 35

Collins, Michael [Leonard Edward] 33, 43, 47

Collins, Mrs [Rosina Jessie] 33, 43

Comper, Sir Ninian 68

Coper, Hans 52, 78

Cotman, John Sell 96

Curtis, Fr Philip 69

Daly, Kathleen 74

Daly, Patrick 74

Daly, Sheila 74

Davage, Rev. William 118

Davies, William Thomas 35

Dean, Alistair Campbell Ross 35

del Nevo, Philip 98

de Quin, Rebecca 128–129

Dick, David Andrew Thomas 35

Dickson, John 81

Doherty, Maureen 120

Edmonds, James Marmaduke 35

Egan, Mark 82

Enders, Caroline 93

Enders, John 41
Fairbanks, Jr., Douglas 41–42, 44
Fitch, Marc 80, 99
Flecker, James Elroy 128
Freeborn, Richard 18, 20, 42
French, John Edward 35
Gaskell, Jane *see* Jane Whitehead
Getty, Paul 40
Gladstone, Gareth Page 35
Glare, Peter 89, 107, 134, 137
Gordon, William Anthony 35
Goudie, Andrew 112, 116–119, 121, 124
Grainger, Alan 82
Grey, Charles 128
Griffith, Thomas Gwynfor 35
Grimshaw, Gladys 98
Grimsley, Thomas 30
Handley, William Richard Cecil 35
Handley-Read, Charles 52, 54
Handley-Read, Lavinia 52
Harber, David 126
Harris, Jose 13
Harrison, Robin 19, 22, 34
Hassall, Tom 75
Haward, Birkin 78
Hawkes, Sonia 81
Helliwell, William 44–45, 85, 105
Helliwell, Mrs [Florence Gladys] 44-45, 85, 105
Herman, Sam 52–53
Hess, Dame Myra 99

Hetherington, Mark 101–102
Hobsbawn, Eric 118
Hockey, Susan 83
Hodcroft, Frederick William 35, 136
Hondius, Frits W. 101
Hooke, Robert 23
Houston, Aubrey Davidson 93
Howlett, Jack 48
Hurst, Ronald 65, 126, 128
Hylson-Smith, Kenneth 102, 107
Jenkins, Brent 84
Jenkins, Roy Harris, The Lord Jenkins of Hillhead 98-99, 102
Jones, Alan 21, 35, 60
Jones, Canon Cheslyn 70–73
Jones, Sir Mark 112, 119, 124
Juel-Jensen, Bent 61
Kelly, Rod 131–132
Kenworthy-Browne, Michael 81
Kirby, Lewis 39–41
Kitching, Roger 47
Knight, Fr Michael R. 87
Knowles, Kenneth Guy Jack Charles 35, 51, 120, 134
Kruger, Nick 75
Lalique, René 52
Lange, Frederick 39, 84, 99, 131
Lankester, Jack 21, 27, 29
La Rue, Hélène 74, 140
Lear, Edward 96

Lefrak, Samuel J. 93
Le Keux, J. 25
Lee, Dame Hermione 38
MacGregor, James John 35
Mackenzie, F. 25
Mackridge, Peter 82
Maclagan, Michael 70
Macmillan, Harold 83, 137
Mapstone, Sally 82
Marshall, Mary 35
Miles, Caroline 90
Morgan, Paul 69, 132
Moore, Temple 59, 68, 72, 91
Morris, William 43
Needham, Arthur Edwin 35
Nizami, Farhan 82, 88
Norrington, A.L.P. 17–19, 21–22, 27, 34
North, Sir Peter 121
Nye, Peter Hague 35
Oakeshott, Walter 20, 23
Osmaston, Firzwalter Camplyon 35
Patterson, David 35, 71
Peacocke, Arthur 88, 90
Philip, Ian Gilbert 35
Pieke, Frank 122
Piper, John 31, 96
Pitt, Charles John William 35
Porter, Simon 73, 78, 81
Purvis, Andy 83
Pusey, Edward Bouverie 67
Pusey, Harold Kenneth 35
Repp, Cathy 140
Repp, Richard ('Dick') 93, 99, 102, 107, 114-115, 118-119, 121, 140

Richards, Donald 73

Rie, Lucie 52

Ramsey, Ian 88, 90, 107

Robertson, James 82

Robbins, Alwyn Rudolph 35

Robb-Smith, Alistair Hamish
    Tearlock 35

Roe, Derek 65, 91, 93, 95,
    112, 132, 137

Rollett, John Sydney 35

Sandford, Sir Folliott 18, 21

Saugman, Per 41–42, 60–61,
    77, 85, 99, 140

Saur, François 101

Savage-Smith, Emilie 101

Sawyer, Walter 126

Schams, Christine 82

Scott, Kate 117

Seligman, Hilda
    (née McDowell) 95

Seligman, Richard 95

Skipper, C. Ian 91

Smith, George 75

Smith, Jennifer *see* Jennifer
    Baines

Southern, Henry Neville 35

Spencer, Marshall
    Macdonald ('Mac') 16, 35

Spiers, John Ashley 35

Stafford, Godfrey 60, 65,
    71, 73, 75, 77, 86, 91–93,
    119, 128, 137

Stafford, Goldy 93

Stranger, Vesla 85

Sturdy, David 102

Sutherland, Donald Martell
    35

Tentrem, Pak 140

Thompson, Gerald Harvey
    35

Thompson, Robert 99

Tiffany, John 69, 107, 132,
    134

Tiffany, Nonny 134

Tinsley, Thomas William 19,
    21, 34, 60-61

Tobin, John 137

Todd, James McLean 35

Treverton, Mildred 52, 77,
    131

Tucker, Richard George 35

Tyler, Godfrey 69, 80, 82

Ursell, Rev. Philip 72, 87

van Heyningen, William
    Edward ('Kits') 16–18,
    20–23, 27, 29–30, 32–33,
    35–36, 38–44, 46, 48, 52,
    54-55, 57, 59-61, 67, 75,
    80, 85, 94, 114, 117, 125

van Heyningen, Ruth
    Eleanor 35, 41, 52, 77, 80,
    99

Vincent, Bob 101

Walshaw, Desmond 51, 74

Ward, Alan 35

Warrell, David 90

Wheare, Kenneth 23

White, Robert (Bob) E. 75

Whitehead (now Gaskell),
    Jane 74

Whittaker, Eric 43, 46, 71-
    73, 77

Wicking, Paul 112

Wigdor, Douglas H. 101, 136

Wigston, F. R. 29

Williams, Arthur Warriner 35

Williamson, Jim 73, 82

Wilner, F de Rohan
    see Vesla Stranger

Wilson, Stuart Swinford 35

Wolton, Suke 126

Wood, Juliet 114

Woolnough, Brian 75

Worthington, Sir Hubert 57

Wren, Christopher

Zernov, Nicolas 35

Zussman, Jack 35

OVERLEAF: Windows above the Van Heyningen Room on the east side of the Blackwell Quad, 2013.

Subscribers

Glenda Abramson
Sayeed Al Noman
Sheila Allcock
Ms Jamie Bartholomew Aller
Masud Ally
Anonymous
Stuart & Miriam Armstrong
Dr Jo Ashbourn
Jennifer Baines
Professor Ros Ballaster
John Barton
Peter Benton
Ms Susan Berrington
Kristina A. Boylan
Christian M. M. Brady
Richard Brett
Dennis Britton
Edward Michael Brookes
Helen W. Brown
David Browning
Samuel J. Bruce
Kenelm O. L. Burridge
Duncan and Karen Campbell
Trevor Campbell Davis
Hung Cheng

Anthony Ka Lun Cheung
Sheungyu Cho
Alan Coates
Jamie Collier
Dr Roger Collins
Tonia Cope Bowley
Jessica Jane Crawford
Gabrielle Cummins
Clíona Dando
    (née Harrison-Barbet)
Gill Davidson
Ian Davies
Jan-Georg Deutsch
Kristina Lunz
Dr James E. Dodd
Ms Maureen Doherty
Professor Michael Dunne
Dr Michael Durkin
Alexander Farquhar
Emma Farrant
Dr Helen Fisher
Hugh Lawrence Flint
Lesley Forbes
Dr Margret Frenz
Edward M. Furgol

Paloma García-Bellido
Dr Adam Gilbertson
Peter Glare
Martin Goodman
Jonathan Gorrie &
    Bronwen Everill
Andrew Goudie
Jane Grayson
Professor T. Gwynfor Griffith
Stephen Michael Gucciardi
Professor Rodney Bruce Hall
Helena Hamerow
Jennifer Handsel
Dr Brian Harrington
T. G. Hassall
Susan Hockey
Ms Suzy Hodge
Fred Hodcroft
Ms Catherine Homsey
Simon Hunt
Dr Michael C. Jacques
Professor Harold W. Jaffe
Wendy R. James
    (Mrs D. H. Johnson)
Dr Hemal Jayasuriya

Dr Brent A. Jenkins
Paul Anthony Johnson
Alan Jones
Mark Jones
Sir Mark Jones
Michel Kenzelmann
Anupum Khaitan
Laura King
Roger Kitching
Yulia Kitova
Professor Nicholas J. Kruger
Flora Lau Pui Yan
Judith Ledger
Anthony Lemon
Karlson K. Leung
Michael Levenstein
Boon Leong Lim
Dr Mary Lloyd
Anastassia Loukina &
    Holger Witte
Ed Macalister-Smith
Oskar MacGregor
Nick Mayhew
Darryl McGill
Bob McLatchie
Michael T. McManus
Janet Mitchell Amara
Prashant Mohan
Hanis Ayuni Mohd Yusof
Dr Charles Mould
Ryan Murray
Poorna Mysoor
Dr Farhan Nizami
Mr Michael G. Noone
Leila Giandoni Ollaik
Joe Olliver
Dr Tom Packer

Barry Parsons
José Patterson
Shaan Pawley
Leanne Peiser
Marina Pérez de Arcos
David Petford
Amanda Petford-Long
Professor James Pettifer
Ms Joanna Pike
Eleanor Pritchard
Pusey House
Dr Romesh Ranawana
Dick Repp
D. S. Richards
Stuart Robinson
Derek Roe
Ján & Martha Sabo
Jessica Sack
Juan Carlos Sainz-Borgo
Lesley Sanderson
Dr Lorenzo Andrea Santorelli
Emilie Savage-Smith
Katharine Scott
Dr Julie Scott-Jackson
Professor William
    Scott-Jackson
Daniel Liam Singer
Derek J. Siveter
John Smallman
Professor George Smith FRS
Laura Soler González
Kuo Tong Soo
Tom Soper
Garrison Sposito
Peter Strong
Dr Alan Taylor
Peter Thompson

Professor Roger Trigg
Jose Carlos Valer Davila
Dr Ruth van Heyningen
Sebastiaan
Kate Venables
Professor Martin Vessey
Rajan Vig
Peter Ward Jones
Dr Katie Warnaby
Mr Alasdair Watson
Simon White
Douglas H. Wigdor
Julia Wigg
Jim Williamson
Anderson M. Winkler
Angeline Wong
Gary Wong Chi Him
Brian E. Woolnough
Wenchuan Wu
Revd Dr Margaret Yee &
    Mr Malcolm Yee
Zixi You

OVERLEAF: The Richard Blackwell Quad,
St Giles site, 2013.

Photograph Credits

Dick Makin Professional Photography, pp. 1, 2–3, 6, 8, 10-11, 12, 64, 81, 106, 108–109, 110, 112 (right), 113, 120, 125, 127, 138, 139, 141, 142, 144–145, 146, 154–155, 156–157, 158–159.

Jeremy Moeran, Studio Edmark, pp. 35, 37, 52, 53, 79, 129 (upper), 130 (upper & lower), 131, 133.

Keith Barnes Photography, pp. 55, 56 (left), 78, 85, 92, 96 (upper & lower), 97, 115, 116.

Oxford, Bodleian Library, pp. 24, 67 (right) [(E) C17:70 OXFORD (12.)]; pp. 26, 67 (left) [Ordnance Survey 1st Edition. Oxfordshire: Sheet XXXIII.15, 1876 (detail)].

Oxford Mail & Times, p. 71 (publ. Oxford Mail, 2 July 1980).

Oxfordshire County Council—Oxfordshire History Centre, p. 27 (right) [OCL 74/2409].

Photoshot License Limited, p. 41.

PS:UNLIMITED, p. 9.

Ruth van Heyningen, pp. 32, 45 (upper & lower), 54, 94.

St Cross College Archives, pp. 25, 28 (upper & lower), 29, 31, 33, 36, 39, 43, 50, 56 (right), 58–59, 62–63, 66, 68, 69, 74 [donated by David Andrews], 76 (upper & lower), 86 (upper), 89, 91, 93, 95 (upper), 95 (lower right), 99, 100 (upper & lower), 101, 103 (lower), 114, 119, 129 (lower), 132, 134, 135, 136, 140.   Peter Benton, p. 122; Sonia Hawkes, pp. 51, 103 (upper); P. C. Masters, p. 30; Joseph Poon [donated by Suzy Roessler], p. 86 (lower); Tim Pound, pp. 27 (left), 40, 102, 104, 112 (left); Derek Roe, p. 95 (lower left); Emilie Savage-Smith, pp. 117, 118.